Bhajan Supplement 2020

Volume 1

Mata Amritanandamayi Center
San Ramon, California, USA

Bhajan Supplement 2020 – Volume 1

Published By:
Mata Amritanandamayi Center
P.O. Box 613
San Ramon, CA 94583-0613, USA

In India:
www.amritapuri.org
inform@amritapuri.org

In Europe:
www.amma-europe.org

In US:
www.amma.org

About Pronunciation

The following key is for the guidance of those who are unfamiliar with the transliteration codes used in this book:

A	-as	a	in America
AI	-as	ai	in aisle
AU	-as	ow	in how
E	-as	e	in they
I	-as	ea	in heat
O	-as	o	in or
U	-as	u	in suit
KH	-as	kh	in Eckhart
G	-as	g	in give
GH	-as	gh	in loghouse
PH	-as	ph	in shepherd
BH	-as	bh	in clubhouse
TH	-as	th	in lighthouse
DH	-as	dh	in redhead
CH	-as	ch-h	in staunch-heart
JH	-as	dge	in hedgehog
Ñ	-as	ny	in canyon
Ṣ	-as	sh	in shine
Ś	-as	c	in efficient
Ṅ	-as	ng	in sing (nasal sound)
V	-as	v	in valley
ZH	-as	rh	in rhythm
R	-as	r	in ride

Vowels with a line on top are pronounced like the vowels listed above but held twice as long.
The letters with dots under them (ṭ, ṭh, ḍ, ḍh, ṇ) are palatal sounds. They are pronounced with the tip of the tongue against the hard palate.

Table of Contents of 3 the Volumes

1. abhayaṅkarī ammē (Malayalam) 2-19
2. abhinnatva torisi (Kannada) 1-19
3. aindezhuttu mandirattin (Tamil) 1-19
4. aisā dil (Hindi) 2-22
5. ājīvanāntam (Tamil version) 1-21
6. akaleyāṇenkilum (Malayāḷam) 1-22
7. akataḷiril aṭimalar (Malayalam) 2-20
8. akatāril azhalinde nizhal (Malayalam) 1-23
9. akhila brahmāṇḍaṅgaḷ (Malayalam) 1-24
10. akumu no youna (Japanese) 2-23
11. alalē lēnidē (Telugu) 1-25
12. āli paṭarum (Malayalam) 2-21
13. ālō kuṭhūna mī (Marathi) 1-27
14. ālōlam-ālōlam (Malayalam) 1-28
15. ambā gauri (Hindi) 2-24
16. ambā jananī (Sanskrit) 2-25
17. ambā kāḷī (Sanskrit) 2-25
18. ambā kṛpā varṣām (Sanskrit) 2-26
19. ammā ammā ammā (Tamil) 2-27
20. ammā dēvi jagadīśvari (Sanskrit) 2-27
21. Amma devi ma (French) 2-28
22. Amma Du bist mein (German) 2-29
23. Amma, hoy me siento lejos (Spanish) 2-30
24. Amma mother of my heart (English) 2-31
25. Amma my heart (English) 2-32
26. amma nin mugdhamām (Malayalam) 2-32
27. amma ninna prēma (Kannada) 1-29

28. Amma okaasam (Japanese) 2-33
29. Amma otzmat (Hebrew) 2-34
30. Amma tu danses (French) 2-35
31. amma unnai ariyāmal (Tamil) 2-36
32. ammā unnanbu (Tamil) 2-37
33. Amma wa itsumo (Japanese) 2-39
34. Amma, you are everything (English) 2-38
35. ammē abhayapradē (Malayalam) 2-39
36. ammē ammē amṛtēśvarī (Malayalam) 2-40
37. ammē ammē ennu (Malayalam) 2-42
38. ammē ammē nitya (Malayalam) 2-43
39. ammē dēvi amṛtēśvarī (Malayalam) 2-44
40. ammē dēvī snēha-svarūpiṇi (Malayalam) 2-45
41. ammē hṛdayēśvari (Malayalam) 2-47
42. ammē hṛdayēśvarī (Malayalam) 2-46
43. ammē karuṇāmayi (Malayalam) 2-48
44. ammē nin māyā (Malayalam) 2-49
45. ammē nin rūpam (Malayalam) 2-50
46. ammē parāśaktī (Malayalam) 2-51
47. ānandam-uḷḷil (Malayalam) 1-30
48. aṅgaḷake hāribandu (Kannada) 1-32
49. añjani putra (Malayalam) 2-52
50. ānondō ānondō (Bengali) 1-33
51. Antakaa Ammalle (Finnish) 2-53
52. antarātmāvil (Malayalam) 1-34
53. arikil-uṇḍenn-amma (Malayalam) 1-35
54. arinda nabarukkō (Tamil) 1-36
55. ārōmal pūmpaitalē (Malayalam) 1-37

56.	ārtta-bandhuvāya dēvi (Malayalam)	1-38
57.	aruṇōdayattiṅkal (Malayalam)	1-39
58.	avanavanār-enn (Malayalam)	2-54
59.	āvō muraḷīdhar (Hindi)	1-40
60.	Awlaadi, awlaadi (Arabic)	2-55
61.	āyēṅgē mērē kānhā āj (Hindi)	1-41
62.	āyiram kātuḷḷa kāḷi (Malayalam)	2-56
63.	āyōrē āyōrē kānhā (Hindi)	1-42
64.	bahū divasāñcī (Marāṭhi)	1-43
65.	bandu chē (Gujarati)	1-45
66.	bārō bārō bālagōpāla (Kannada)	2-57
67.	bhagavan ham par (Hindi)	2-58
68.	bhagavān kahāṅ (Hindi)	1-46
69.	bhajeham gaṇēśam (Sanskrit)	2-59
70.	bhajlē rām rām rām (Hindi)	1-47
71.	bhakti dē mā (Hindi)	1-49
72.	bhayamannadi (Telugu)	2-61
73.	bhītiyilāyen manam (Malayalam)	2-62
74.	birahō āgune (Bengali)	1-50
75.	bōlo śyām rādhē rādhē (Hindi)	1-51
76.	Celebramos la vida (Spanish)	2-63
77.	cēsēdi nīvamma (Telugu)	1-52
78.	chod de mānase (Odiya version)	1-53
79.	cilambōli kēṭṭuvō (Malayalam)	2-64
80.	cinmay sundar (Marathi)	1-54
81.	citaykkarikil (Malayalam)	1-55
82.	Cógeme la mano (Spanish)	2-65
83.	Cuando la madre tierra (Spanish)	2-66

84. ḍamaruka-nātha (Sanskrit) 2-67
85. dē darśan mā (Odiya version) 1-57
86. Desire leads to anger (English) 1-57
87. Devi awaken your children (English) 2-68
88. dēvi mahāśaktī (Malayalam) 2-68
89. dēvi mātē durgē (Malayalam) 2-69
90. dil kō banā dō (Hindi) 1-58
91. dīnabandhō (Sanskrit) 2-70
92. Don't let me waste this life (English) 1-59
93. Du er mit smukke hjem (Danish) 2-71
94. ē amma! (Telugu) 1-60
95. ē duniyā hai (Punjabi) 1-61
96. ēk dīp jalāyē ham (Hindi) 1-62
97. ēk ēk jap sē (Hindi) 2-71
98. ēk vacani ēk bāṇi (Marathi) 1-64
99. eḷimayānavaḷ (Tamil) 2-72
100. Em habria ahava (Hebrew) 2-73
101. Engulfed in this dark world (English) 2-74
102. en manaceppil (Malayalam) 2-75
103. enne nayikkuvān (Malayalam) 2-76
104. ennu kēḷkkum (Malayalam) 2-77
105. entinō vēṇḍi (Malayalam) 2-78
106. entinu śokam (Telugu version) 1-65
107. entu colvān-uddhavare (Malayalam) 2-79
108. Eons of lifetimes (English) 1-66
109. Epsahna stin nihta (Greek) 2-80
110. gaṇēśa namaḥ ōm (Odiya version) 1-66
111. gaṇēśa siddhi dātā (Hindi) 1-67

112.	giri vana puri (Kannada)	1-68
113.	gōkulanāthā gōpakumārā (Tamil)	1-69
114.	gōpālak bāsurī (Hindi)	1-70
115.	Gotts himmel (German)	2-82
116.	gōvarddhanam uyartti (Malayalam)	2-84
117.	Hakuna matata (Swahili)	2-85
118.	Hana mo tori mo (Japanese)	2-86
119.	hara hara śiva śiva (Malayalam)	2-87
120.	hōli āyī dēkhō (Hindi)	2-89
121.	hōli āyi khuśiyāṅ (Hindi)	1-71
122.	Hør Gud, hvor (Danish)	2-90
123.	hṛdayam dravicc-ozhukum (Malayalam)	1-73
124.	hṛdayattin aṭittaṭṭil (Malayalam)	2-91
125.	hṛdinivāsi (Kannada)	1-74
126.	Illumina el mey camí (Catalan)	2-92
127.	Ilumina ilumina (Spanish)	2-93
128.	indranīladyutim (Sanskrit)	2-94
129.	indu habba (Baḍuga)	1-75
130.	indukalā-dhara (Sanskrit)	1-76
131.	In every heart (English)	2-95
132.	ini oru janmam (Tamil version)	1-77
133.	innentē vannilla (Malayalam)	1-78
134.	iṇṭilōkki (Telugu)	1-80
135.	Io sono una bolla (Italian)	2-95
136.	iruḷil ninnuṭal (Malayalam)	1-81
137.	iruḷ māri teḷiyānāyi (Malayalam)	1-82
138.	I see in this dark night (English)	2-96
139.	jab se pāvan (Hindi)	2-97

140. jagadambā prēmānē (Marathi) 1-83
141. jagadīśvarī mā (Malayalam) 2-98
142. jagatanātha (Odiya) 1-84
143. jag spandan (Hindi) 2-102
144. Jai jai mukunda (Spanish) 2-103
145. jaya jaya śankara (Kannada) 1-85
146. jaya rama rama ram (French) 2-99
147. jay jay dēvi (Sanskrit) 2-100
148. jay rām sītāpatē (Sanskrit) 2-100
149. Je suis un rayon (French) 2-101
150. jīvitam-ennoru tuṭarkatha (Malayalam) 1-86
151. jīvita ommē (Kannada) 1-87
152. jñāna-dīpam (Malayalam) 1-88
153. jōt jalālē rām (Hindi) 1-90
154. kaisā nāc nacāyā (Hindi) 1-92
155. kāj karō (Hindi) 1-93
156. kali devi jaganmata (Sanskrit) 2-104
157. Kāḷī dēvī, mother to me (English) 1-94
158. kāḷi kāḷi kāḷi kālasvarūpiṇi (Telugu) 1-95
159. kāḷi kāḷi kapālini (Sanskrit) 2-105
160. kāḷī karāḷī mahāśakti (Sanskrit) 2-106
161. Kali mata zai (Chinese) 2-107
162. kamanīya-rūpan (Malayalam) 1-96
163. kaṇā kaṇā (Marathi) 1-98
164. kāṇān-uzharunna (Malayalam) 2-107
165. Kang a yo i wei (Chinese) 2-109
166. kanivoṭakaṭṭuka (Malayalam) 2-109
167. kaṇṇane kāṇān (Malayalam) 2-111

168.	kaṇṇan-en cārattu (Malayalam)	1-100
169.	kaṇṇā nin vēṇu (Malayalam)	1-99
170.	kaṇṇā nī ōṭi vāyō (Malayalam)	2-112
171.	kaṇṇirkkaṭalin karayil (Malayalam)	1-101
172.	kaṇṇunnīru tumbi (Badaga)	2-113
173.	karaḷ niraññu (Malayalam)	1-102
174.	karayāt-endōmana (Malayalam)	2-114
175.	karimukil varṇṇā (Malayalam)	2-115
176.	kar-lē dhyān tu bandē (Hindi)	1-103
177.	kārmukil varṇṇande līlakaḷ (Malayalam)	1-105
178.	kārtikēya subrahmaṇya (Telugu)	1-106
179.	karuṇārdra mānasē (Malayalam)	2-117
180.	karuṇayinda (Kannada)	1-107
181.	kāruṇyarūpiṇi ammē nin (Malayalam)	2-118
182.	kāttaruḷvāy dēvi (Tamil)	2-119
183.	kātyāyani dēvi (Hindi)	2-121
184.	Kmo navad hatoe (Hebrew)	2-122
185.	Kokoroyo nanio (Japanese)	2-122
186.	Kom hjem mit barn (Danish)	2-124
187.	Kom tillsammans (Swedish)	2-125
188.	koṇḍāṭṭamām (Tamil)	2-126
189.	krishna krishna jay jay (Chinese)	2-128
190.	kṛṣṇaghanā rē (Marathi)	1-109
191.	kṛṣṇā kṛṣṇā dēvakī nandana (Sanskrit)	2-127
192.	kṛṣṇā, nī ennil (Malayalam)	2-129
193.	kuṭilam-ākum (Malayalam)	1-110
194.	laḷitāmbikē ammē (Malayalam)	2-130
195.	Lämmössä tuulen (Finnish)	2-131

196. Liebe Amma (German) 2-132
197. Liefde voor God (Dutch) 2-132
198. Llum de la llum (Catalan) 2-133
199. Love is you, love is me (English) 2-134
200. Lurreko mantu leuna (Basque) 2-135
201. lūtayil ninnu (Malayalam) 1-111
202. Maadare man (Persian) 2-136
203. māḍī tārī (Gujarati) 1-112
204. Mā inspire l'amour (French) 2-137
205. maiyyājī huṇ mērā (Punjabi) 1-114
206. Mā kālī devī (French) 2-138
207. mākhan cōr (Hindi) 1-115
208. manasā... cēyavē (Telugu) 1-116
209. manasē ō manasē (Kannada) 2-140
210. manasigē kaccikoḷuva āse (Kannada) 1-117
211. manassil menayunna (Malayalam) 2-141
212. mānava janmavu (Kannada) 1-118
213. manavē kāraṇa (Kannada) 2-142
214. manidā manidā (Tamil) 1-120
215. maṇi-māṇiku (Hindi) 1-119
216. maṇṇaiyaḷakka (Tamil) 1-121
217. manōdarppaṇattil (Malayalam) 1-122
218. man tō bandhi (Hindi) 1-124
219. manvā rē tu (Hindi) 1-125
220. mā ō mā mārī (Gujarati) 1-126
221. maraṇattin-oru cuvaṭu (Malayalam) 1-127
222. mārgamulu enni (Telugu) 1-129
223. mā śakti hai (Punjabi) 2-143

224.	māyai adu niṙaindirukkum (Tamil)	2-144
225.	māye tanna (Kannada)	1-130
226.	mērī dēvīmā (Punjabi)	1-131
227.	Mir, lyubov' (Russian)	2-145
228.	mōr paṅkh (Hindi)	1-132
229.	Mother divine (English)	2-146
230.	Mother ocean (English)	2-147
231.	Moye serce byotsya (Russian)	2-148
232.	mṛtyuñjaya hara (Sanskrit)	2-151
233.	mukiloḷi niram (Malayalam)	1-134
234.	muḷam taṇḍil (Malayalam)	2-152
235.	muruga muruga (Malayalam)	2-153
236.	muttu muttu māriyamma (Tamil)	1-136
237.	nācē kānuḍō nācē (Gujarati)	1-137
238.	nā kaṇṭiki velugu (Telugu)	2-154
239.	Nakhtalifu (Arabic-Egyptian)	2-154
240.	nalvazhikāṭṭiṭu jayalakṣmi (Tamil)	2-156
241.	ñān aṙiyunnu (Malayalam)	2-157
242.	nandalālā yadu nandalālā (Hindi)	1-138
243.	narajanmōgu (Tulu)	1-139
244.	navvu navvu (Telugu)	1-141
245.	nēh mujhē dō (Hindi)	1-142
246.	nel tarum (Tamil)	1-143
247.	nīlāñjana mizhi (Kannada version)	1-145
248.	nīlō nīlō nīlōnē (Telugu)	1-146
249.	nin malarvāṭiyil (Malayalam)	2-158
250.	ninna naguvu (Kannada)	1-147
251.	ninna nirmala (Kannada)	1-148

252.	ninnapāda sēvēmāḍalū (Kannada)	2-159
253.	nin pādapadmattil aṇayān (Malayalam)	2-160
254.	ninu kīrtimpa (Telugu)	1-149
255.	nīr bharā (Hindi)	2-161
256.	niścala koḷada (Kannada)	1-150
257.	niṣphala-svapnattil (Malayalam)	2-162
258.	nit din tarsē (Hindi)	1-151
259.	nityānandattil (Malayalam)	2-163
260.	nī viral toṭṭāl (Malayalam)	1-144
261.	Noor a veen (Irish)	2-164
262.	nṛttamāḍu (Malayalam)	1-152
263.	O Amma, please come (English)	2-165
264.	Oh mind of mine (English)	2-166
265.	Oi Äiti (Finnish)	2-167
266.	ō man mālik (Hindi)	1-154
267.	ō mā ō mā (Hindi)	2-168
268.	ō mā sab lōkōṅ (Hindi)	2-168
269.	ōmkāra divya porūḷe 47 (Malayalam)	ODP-19
270.	ōmkāra divya porūḷe 48 (Malayalam)	ODP-33
271.	ōmkāra divya porūḷe 49 (Malayalam)	ODP-48
272.	ōmkāra divya porūḷe 50 (Malayalam)	ODP-63
273.	ōmkāra divya porūḷe 51 (Malayalam)	ODP-78
274.	ōmkāra divya porūḷe 52 (Malayalam)	ODP-94
275.	ōmkāra divya porūḷe 53 (Malayalam)	ODP-110
276.	ōmkāra divya porūḷe 54 (Malayalam)	ODP-126
277.	ōmkāra divya porūḷe 55 (Malayalam)	ODP-143
278.	ōmkāra divya porūḷe 56 (Malayalam)	ODP-160
279.	ōmkāra divya porūḷe 57 (Malayalam)	ODP-177

280. ōmkāra divya porūḷe 58 (Malayalam) ODP-195
281. ōmkāra divya porūḷe 59 (Malayalam) ODP-213
282. ōmkāra divya porūḷe 60 (Malayalam) ODP-231
283. ōmkāra divya porūḷe 61 (Malayalam) ODP-249
284. ōmkāra divya porūḷe 62 (Malayalam) ODP-267
285. ōmkāra divya porūḷe 63 (Malayalam) ODP-286
286. ōmkāra divya porūḷe 64 (Malayalam) ODP-305
287. ōmkāra divya porūḷe 65 (Malayalam) ODP-325
288. ōmkāra divya porūḷe 66 (Malayalam) ODP-345
289. ōmkāra svaramezhum (Malayalam) 1-155
290. ōm namō bhagavatē rudrāya (Sanskrit) 2-169
291. O Mother, when will I live your dream (English) 1-156
292. O my dear Kali (English) 2-170
293. onnum uriyāṭān (Malayalam) 2-171
294. On the banks of the river (English) 1-157
295. oru mazhakkālavum (Malayalam) 2-172
296. oru naḷil ñān en (Kannada version) 1-158
297. oru nerippōṭ-eriyunnu (Malayalam) 2-173
298. oru nōṭṭam-ēkāttat-entē (Malayalam) 1-158
299. oru piñcupaitalām (Malayalam) 2-175
300. oru vitumbal mātram (Malayalam) 1-159
301. Ote bondie (Kreole) 2-176
302. pāhimām pāhimām (Sanskrit) 2-176
303. pāhimām paramēśvarī (Malayalam) 1-160
304. pañcākṣara mandirattai (Tamil) 2-178
305. pannagaśāyi pārthasārathi (Kannada) 1-161
306. pantaḷa rājā ayyappā (Malayalam) 2-179
307. parandu virindu (Tamil) 2-180

308.	Pikimusta taivas (Finnish)	2-181
309.	pittā endrazhaittālum (Tamil)	1-162
310.	prabhu bin (Hindi)	2-183
311.	prabhuji tērā darśan (Hindi)	1-164
312.	prēmadondu (Kannada)	2-184
313.	prēma-gaṅgē ammē (Malayalam)	1-166
314.	prēmattin tūlika (Malayalam)	2-185
315.	prēm sē gāō (Hindi)	1-165
316.	puṭṭa puṭṭa kṛṣṇā (Kannada)	1-167
317.	rāma rāma jaya (Sanskrit)	2-186
318.	rām hamārē śyām hamārē (Hindi)	1-168
319.	rām hī rām (Hindi)	1-169
320.	rām rām rām (Sanskrit)	2-187
321.	raṅg jā tu maiyyā (Punjabi)	1-170
322.	ravikula-tilaka (Sanskrit)	1-172
323.	Reflect on life (English)	1-173
324.	ruṭhā hai kyōṅ mērē lāl (Hindi)	1-174
325.	sācō tērō nām (Hindi)	1-175
326.	sadāśivā mahēśvarā (Malayalam)	1-176
327.	sādi tōjāle (Tulu)	1-177
328.	śakti tū sab jīv (Hindi)	1-178
329.	samasta līḷārē (Odiya)	1-179
330.	śambho śaṅkara (Tamil)	2-188
331.	Seigneur Krishna (French)	2-189
332.	Sento le onde (Italian)	2-190
333.	śēr tē savār āyī (Punjabi)	1-181
334.	Shénshèng Mŭqīn (Chinese)	2-191
335.	Show me your real form (English)	2-192

336.	śibjē bhōlā (Bengali)	1-182
337.	siṭrinbam nāḍum (Tamil)	1-183
338.	Sitting in the dark (English)	2-193
339.	śiva mahādēva (Sanskrit)	2-193
340.	śiva śiva śiva śiva uraittiḍuvāyē (Tamil)	1-184
341.	śivōham śivōham (Hindi)	1-185
342.	Somos todos um (Portuguese)	2-194
343.	śrī rāma rāma raghurāma (Sanskrit)	2-195
344.	śrīśailavāsini (Sanskrit)	2-196
345.	sukhattilum (Malayalam)	2-197
346.	sumadhura sundara (Sanskrit)	1-186
347.	sun mēri mayyā (Hindi)	1-188
348.	sun sun mā (Hindi)	2-198
349.	Szukam cie w nocy (Polish)	2-199
350.	tabōnām (Bengali)	1-189
351.	taka dhimi taka jaṇu (Malayalam)	2-200
352.	tallī vallī kalpavallī (Telugu)	1-190
353.	tām tittām tey tey (Malayalam)	2-201
354.	tañjamena vandōm (Tamil)	1-191
355.	tannana tannana (English)	2-203
356.	tāyē unai (Tamil)	2-203
357.	teccippū piccippū (Malayalam)	1-192
358.	tēḍi tēḍi (Tamil)	1-194
359.	tellaccīra kaṭṭināvē (Telugu)	2-204
360.	tērā darśan karnē (Punjabi)	1-195
361.	tērē vicc maiyā (Punjabi)	1-196
362.	Thank you for this life (English)	2-206
363.	The pendulum of life (English)	1-197

364.	The world reels (English)	1-198
365.	tīn guṇōṅ kī (Hindi)	1-199
366.	toṭṭuṇartti (Tamil)	1-200
367.	tuḷaśīmāḷā gaḷā (Marathi)	1-201
368.	tuḷasīmālayāy (Malayalam)	2-206
369.	tūyi kālō (Bengali)	1-203
370.	tyāga diyā tūnē (Hindi)	1-204
371.	ulagam oru pūntōṭṭam (Tamil)	1-205
372.	ulakattin ādhāra (Tamil version)	1-206
373.	umaye uḷḷil (Malayalam)	2-207
374.	vāgiś nāgēś (Hindi)	1-207
375.	vāṇi sarasvati (Malayalam)	2-208
376.	vānōrum (Tamil)	1-208
377.	vattātta snēhattin (Malayalam)	1-209
378.	vāzhkeyenum paḍaku (Tamil)	1-210
379.	vēlavanē śakti (Tamil)	2-209
380.	vēlmurugā vēlmurugā (Tamil)	1-212
381.	veṇṇai uṇṇum (Tamil)	2-210
382.	viḍarātta tāmara (Kannada version)	1-214
383.	vinati hamare tune (Odiya version)	1-213
384.	Vind de vrede (Dutch)	2-211
385.	viṭhala viṭhala viṭhala viṭhala (Konkani)	1-214
386.	viṭhal hari viṭhal nām gajari (Marathi)	1-216
387.	vittumundā (Telugu)	1-217
388.	Vlepo thavmata (Greek)	2-212
389.	Warum suchen wir (German)	2-214
390.	yadukulam (Malayalam)	1-218

abhinnatva torisi (Kannada)

abhinnatva tōrisi abhimānava tyajisi
adharma toḷagisi kalmaṣa nīguva
jaya jaya sanātani, jaya sanātani ṛṣiyē

Practice non-duality and abandon false pride. Avoid unrighteousness and remove impurities. Victory to the Goddess! Hail to the eternal lineage of seers!

bhaktiya pasarisi lōka sangrahava beḷasi
jñāna beḷagisi ānanda-svādisuva
jaya jaya sanātani, jaya sanātani ṛṣiyē

Spread the fragrance of devotion, and promote the welfare of the world. Illumine your mind with wisdom and relish divine bliss. Victory to the Goddess! Hail to the eternal lineage of seers!

bhayava dūragoḷisi sāntvanava upadēśisi
samsāra bhēdisi paramārtha bōdhisu
jaya jaya sanātani, jaya sanātani ṛṣiyē

Keep fear away and console others with words of wisdom. Transcend the cycle of life and death, and impart supreme wisdom to others. Victory to the Goddess! Hail to the eternal lineage of seers!

aindezhuttu mandirattin (Tamil)

namperumānē pōttri
mativaṇṇanē pōttri
siddhanāthanē pōttri
vāmadēvanē pōttri
yajñarūpanē pōttri

namaḥ śivāya pōttri pōttri

Salutations to the Lord, to the One with a moon-like complexion. Salutations to the Lord of the mind and to the preserving aspect of Lord Shiva. Salutations to You whose form is sacrifice. Salutations to Lord Shiva!

aindezhuttu mandirattin ezhuttellām śivamē
aiyamindṛi solpavarkku anaittumingu śivamē

Each syllable of the five-lettered mantra (Na-Ma-Shi-Va-Ya) is Shiva. For those who chant it with confidence, everything here is Shiva.

edarkku inda pirappu? enḍru ariya nīyum virumbu
eppōdu irappu? enbad-iraivan avan poruppu
pirappu irappu aruttiḍum pirai sūḍan avan padangaḷ
pirazhāmal ninaikka ninaikka muḍindiṭum munvinaigaḷ

Long to know why you have this human birth. It is God's responsibility to determine your time of death. Lord Shiva, who wears the crescent moon on His head, can cut the cycle of birth and death. Constant contemplation on His holy feet will end all your karma.

ōm namaḥ śivāya ōm namaḥ śivāya
ōm namaḥ śivāya ōm namaḥ śivāya

Salutations to Shiva, the auspicious One!

kattradu kaḍukaḷavu eninum garvam kaḍal aḷavu
pettradu ūraḷavu eninum āsai ulagam aḷavu
kattraduvum pettraduvum kaḍaisi varai varumō?
kalangāmal manamē dinam uraittiḍu śivanāmam

Though all your learning is as small as a mustard seed, your ego is as big as the ocean. Though your wealth is as big as a city, your desire is as big as the world. Will what you have learned and earned accompany you until the very end? O mind! don't worry. Chant Lord Shiva's name every day.

vāzhum manidar ninaippaduṇḍu maraṇam tanakku illai
māṇḍavarai kaṇḍum kūḍa mayakkam teḷivadillai
tillaiyil nindrāḍiḍum naṭarājan avan pugazhai
dinamum kēṭka ninaivil nilaikka aganḍriḍum ariyāmai

The living think that death is not for them. Even after seeing the dead, they remain deluded. Lord Nataraja dances the cosmic dance in the Thillai temple (a temple in Tamil Nadu, South India). By listening, reflecting and continuously contemplating on his divine glory, your ignorance will vanish.

ājīvanāntam (Tamil version)

āyuḷvarai nān vaṇankiḍuvēn
ātankam indru nī tīrttiḍuvāy
ādiparāśakti āna dēvi
ākulam nīkki aruḷ purivāy

vēṇḍuvadellām nalkum ammā
pērūkaḷ aḷikkum annaiyum nī
ellōrai tānkiḍum śaktiyum nī
śankari nityamē sattiyamē

tyāgankaḷ ettanai seygirēn nān
tāmadam ēnō kaṇ malara
tāyē nin māyaiyil āzhttiḍādē
tāmarai pādam paṇivēn enḍrum

akaleyāṇenkilum (Malayāḷam)

akaleyāṇenkilum ariyunnu ammē nin
avirāma snēha pravāham
arikiluṇden manam ariyunnuvō ninde
maḍiyil ñān talacāycc-iruppū

Though You are far away, I feel the incessant flow of Your love. Do you know that my heart is beside You, and I rest my head in Your lap?

kanivinde pālāzhi alatallum mizhikaḷāl
enne talōḍunna nēram
karayukayalla ñān ennālum-en kaṇkaḷ
tōrāte peytēy-irippū

Your gaze caresses me with waves of compassion. I am not crying, though my eyes rain tears.

amma-tan prēmam-en ālambanam
ammayen jīvita rāgāmṛtam

Mother's love is my support. She is the sweetness of my life's melody.

sukha-duḥkha-tirakaḷil alayaḍicc-en janmam
oḍuvil-aṇayunna tīram
akaleyallennu ñān ariyunnu amma-tan
nalamezhum puñciri kāṇkē

You are the shore that my life, agitated by the waves of pain and pleasure, finally attains. When I see Your compassionate smile, O Mother, I know that I am not far away.

vāriy-eḍuttenne mārōḍ-aṇacc-amma
kātil mozhiyunnat-entum
vākkukaḷ-illātta bhāṣayum-illātta
nirmala prēma sangītam!

O Mother, You draw me into Your arms and whisper in my ear. All that You say is the pure music of love, beyond words or language.

akatāril azhalinde nizhal (Malayalam)

akatāril azhalinde nizhal paratti-kaṇṇan
akalattil eṅgō maraññu-ninnu
nirupama-prēmattāl rādha-tan mānasam
alakaṭal pōlārttu-kēṇu dinam
alakaṭal pōlārttu-kēṇu dinam
kaṇṇā... kaṇṇā... kaṇṇā... kaṇṇā...

Sorrowful shadows enveloped Radha's mind as Lord Krishna remained hidden far away. Her heart cried out in the pain of unparalleled love, like the unceasing waves of the roaring ocean. O Krishna...

virahattin rōdanam kēṭṭatilla nāthan
kanivinde kuḷir-māri tūkiyilla
kamanīya-rūpane kaṇikāṇān vembumī-
hṛdaya-nikuñje aṇaññatilla
hṛdaya-nikuñje aṇaññatilla
kaṇṇā... kaṇṇā... kaṇṇā... kaṇṇā...

The Lord did not hear her longing cry. He did not pour down the soothing shower of His compassion. He did not enter the grove of Radha's pining heart. O Krishna...

priya-rāgam pāḍi uṇarttiṭāte
oru puñciri-pūpōlum viṭarttiṭāte
onnum-ariyātta bhāvattil akannu-nilppū
ī paribhavam-ennōḍ-entināṇō?
ī paribhavam-ennōḍ-entināṇō?
kaṇṇā... kaṇṇā... kaṇṇā... kaṇṇā...

You do not awaken my heart with Your song. You do not awaken even a smile within me. You stay away as if unaware of my agony. Why are you so upset with me? O Krishna...

akhila brahmāṇḍaṅgaḷ (Malayalam)

akhila brahmāṇḍaṅgaḷ ñoṭiyil
raciccitum amṛtasvarūpiṇī dēvī
vinatayām sutayende bhavabhayam nīkkuvān
tuṇakkyāttat-entē sarvēśī – ammē
tuṇakkyāttat-entē sarvēśī

O Devi, your nature is immortal bliss. You created all the universes in a single moment. This child of yours is very scared of this world and all its perils. Why do you not come to my aid and remove my fear? O Mother, O Empress of this Universe, why do you not come to help me?

karuṇāmbudhē ninkal aṇayān kotikkunna
taraḷāmbu-bindu ñān-ammē
akhilātma-nāyakī sakalārtti-hāriṇī
agatikkor-avalambam-aruḷū – ammē

agatikkor-avalambam-aruḷū

You are an ocean of compassion, O mother. I am a tiny drop of water that longs to reach and merge into You. Queen of every soul, destroyer of every desire, O Mother, please give refuge to this destitute child!

mizhinīr kaṭal-tannil uyarum tirakaḷil
citari terikkum-en cittam
ninavinde taṇalil nī maravi-tan nizhalattu
verute raciccoru citram – ammē
verute raciccoru citram

My heart shatters in the waves arising in the ocean of my tears. In the shade of remembrance, in the shadows of forgetfulness, You have playfully drawn a picture, O Mother!

kadanattil-urukumī hṛdayattil-uraviṭum
virahārtta mōhaṅgal mātram
karutunnivaḷ nin caraṇāmbujē cērnnu
caritārtthayākuvān nityam – ammē
caritārtthayākuvān nityam

My heart melts in the fire of separation and longs to be one with You. I long to merge into your lotus feet and attain eternal fulfilment, O Mother!

alalē lēnidē (Telugu)

alalē lēnidē kaḍalē lēdu
ceṭlu lēnidē aḍavē lēdu
cintalu lēnidē manasē lēdu
manasu lēnidē jagamē lēdu

The ocean cannot be without waves. A forest cannot be without trees. A mind cannot be without thoughts. There can be no world without the mind.

dṛṣṭi mārcukō dhīrā
sṛṣṭi nī dṛṣṭi sṛṣṭirā

Change your perspective, O man of strong intellect. This creation is only a projection of your mind.

jagamē cintalu terapai bommalu
ūhala alalu vacci pōvunu
cintalu rāni anṭaka cūḍu
gatamu tavvaku bhavita allaku

The world is just thoughts appearing as images on the screen (of consciousness). The waves of thoughts come and go. Watch them without attachment. Forget the past. Don't weave the future.

ī kṣaṇamē unnadi sākṣigā cūḍu
cintala naḍuma sandu unnadi
ā sandu ninḍā maunam unnadi
maunamu lōnē amma unnadi

The present moment is all you have. Be like a witness. Complete silence fills the gap between the thoughts. In that silence and stillness, the divine mother resides and peace prevails.

ammani cēru śāntini pondu
śānti... śānti... śānti... śānti...
śānti... śānti... śānti...

Reach Mother, obtain peace! Peace... peace... peace... peace...

ālō kuṭhūna mī (Marathi)

ālō kuṭhūna mī jātō kōṭhē
dēha manāśī kāy mājhē nātē
umajalē nā kāhī malā
gurucaraṇī māthā mī ṭhēvilā

Where have I come from? Where am I going? What is my relation to this body and mind? I have not understood any of this. I rest my head at the Guru's feet. I surrender to the Guru.

mī paṇācē manā kautuka mōṭhē
kṣaṇa puḍhilā āhē hātī kōṭhē
khēḷa manācē hē nakō malā
gurucaraṇī māthā mī ṭhēvilā

The mind is too fond of the ego. Even the next moment is out of our hands. I'm done with the mind's play. I rest my head at the Guru's feet.

śabda sparśādī mṛgajaḷē
duḥkhaca sadā yātūna miḷē
bhulūna yannā jīva thaklā
gurucaraṇī māthā mī ṭhēvilā

Sound, touch and all sensory pleasures are mirages that bring only sorrow. I am tired of their delusion. I rest my head at the Guru's feet.

ahankārācē ōjhē mōṭhē
gurucaraṇī karūnī rītē
gurupadī jīva hā vāhilā
gurucaraṇī māthā mī ṭhēvilā

I lay my selfishness at the Guru's feet and surrender my life to the Guru. I rest my head at the Guru's feet.

ālōlam-ālōlam (Malayalam)

ālōlam-ālōlam-āḍān
ammē ā tiru-maṭiyil-uraṅgān
ā mṛdu-cumbanam-ēlkkān
ammē ā tiru-mārilāy cāyān

Cradle me in Your arms, O Mother. Let me sleep in Your lap. Let me know the softness of Your kiss. Let me lie on Your shoulder.

kotiyōṭe kotiyōṭe nilppū ammē
ā prēma-sāyūjyam-ariyān
ā nitya-nirvṛti ariyān ammē
ā tiru-mozhikaḷ śravikkān
ā tiru-mozhikaḷ śravikkān

I long for the liberating power of Your love. I long to realize the eternal bliss that is Your nature. I long to hear the sweet melody of Your voice.

kātōrttu kātōrtt-irippū ammē
ā prēma-kathakaḷ ariyān
ā prēmapuñciri tennal
enne tazhuki talōṭi urakkān
enne tazhuki talōṭi urakkān

O Mother, I listen intently to tales of Your love. I yearn for the gentle breeze of Your loving smile to caress me to sleep.

ariyāte ariyāte ozhuki – nin prēma
kallōlini āyiṭuvān
ā prēma-sāgara-tīrē nityam
aṇayān koticc-ivaḷ nilppū

aṇayān koticc-ivaḷ nilppū

I long to be a surging stream of love that merges in the ocean of Your love. How I long to reach the shore of the ocean of Your love!

anantānandam ēkīṭān ammē
kanivūrum nayanaṅgaḷ uḷḷil
uṇarēṇam-ennennum-uḷḷam
ātma-sūrya-praśōbha ēkīṭān
ātma-sūrya-praśōbha ēkīṭān

O Mother, please bestow infinite bliss on me. Awaken my inner self under Your compassionate glance. May the Self shine with the glory of the sun.

amma ninna prēma (Kannada)

amma ninna prēma gīte hēgē hāḍali
ninna pāra daivi guṇava hēgē varṇisali

Mother, how can I sing a song of devotion to You? How can I describe your infinite divine qualities?

hagalu iruḷu makkaḷa santaisu-ttiruvē
jātimata bhēda vennade samadṛṣṭi tōruvē
ninna prēma kāruṇyava hēgē hogaḷali
ninna sṛṣṭi kāraṇavu lōka saṅgrahavē

Day and night, You tend Your children, showing equal love to all regardless of caste or creed. How can I praise Your love and compassion? Your advent on the earth is to protect the world.

namma kai biḍabēḍa anātharāgisa bēḍa
dura māḍalu bēḍa prēmakaruṇe tōramma

ninna maḍilē namage āśrayavamma

Mother, please do not abandon me. Do not make me an orphan. Do not leave my side. Shower love and compassion on me. Your lap is my sole refuge.

prēma karuṇe anukampa nammalli mūḍisi
jagad-upakārava gaiva samskāra tumbihē
ninna caraṇa kamalad-aḍige āśrayavanīḍi
nammannu ninnalle aikya goḷisu

By awakening love and compassion within us, You make us fit to serve the world. Give us refuge at Your holy feet and finally make us merge in You.

ānandam-uḷḷil (Malayalam)

ānandam-uḷḷil-āṇennu collumbōzhum-
ā-bōdham-uḷḷil-oṭṭilla tellum
vēdānta-śāstram manaḥ-pāṭham-āyiṭām
tattva-sākṣātkāra pāta dūram

We proclaim that happiness is within us, but we have yet to realize the bliss. We have thorough knowledge of Vedic scriptures, but we are far from realizing the Truth declared by the Vedas.

satyam jñānam anantam brahma
satyam jñānam anantam brahma

Brahman is truth, knowledge, infinity.

māyatan māntrika-jālam mahāścaryam
ōrttiṭunn-illahō nitya-satyam
rāga-bhōgaṅgaḷām vahniyil hā kaṣṭam

hōmippū śrēṣṭham-ī-martya-janmam

Wondrous is the magic of illusion. We forget the eternal truth. The fire of insatiable desires and sense pleasures consumes our noble human birth.

bhōgāśa nīṅgaṇam bhakti vaḷarēṇam
sadguru kāruṇyam nēṭīṭēṇam
nisvārtthar-ākēṇam nirmalar-ākēṇam
sarvadā nanmakaḷ kāṇākēṇam

Our devotion must grow and our desires should diminish. We must earn the compassionate grace of the Satguru. Becoming selfless and pure, we will perceive goodness everywhere.

īśvara-prēma nilāvu teḷiyēṇam
hṛttaṭam nannāyi turanniṭēṇam
prēmam-ā jīva-bhāvatte haniccitum
ātma-svarūpattil-ārdram-ākkum

Our hearts should become radiant in the moonlight of God's love. We must open wide the doors of our heart. Pure love of God will annihilate our ego. Only thus are we established in the nature of the Self.

anyarum tānum-illadvaita-bhāvam-ī-
ajñāna nāśattin hētuvākum
prārabdha-śēṣam-ā dēham kozhiññiṭum
jñānattil-āgāmi-sañcitam pōl

Our ignorance will vanish in the knowledge of non-duality when we realize that the supreme Self alone exists. Our knowledge of the Self will liberate us from any further births to experience the fruits of all our accumulated karmas.

aṅgaḷake hāribandu (Kannada)

aṅgaḷake hāri bandu kāḷanondu hekki hakki
purr entu hāri hōguvante
jīvanada śālegindu jīviyondu igo bande
bēga bēga pāṭha kaliyuve – nā
bēga bēga pāṭha kaliyuve

Like the little bird, descending in the front yard, picks up a grain and flies off with a purr, I have come to the school of life; I will learn my lessons quickly.

vēda mantra gaṇṭe ghōṣa hakki hāḍu idara maddhyē
dhyāna japa sāṅgavāgali
puḷakagoṇḍu nasukinalle araḷi ninta kusumavāgi
pūjegendu mīsaliruve – nā
pūjegendu mīsaliruve – nā

In the midst of Vedic chanting, temple bells and bird song, may my sadhana progress smoothly. May I be the flower that blooms in the very early morning, and may I be a flower meant for Your worship.

vītarāga dvēṣa klēśa aṇṭu naṇṭu gōjalilla
niṣkaḷaṅka manava paḍeyuve – nā
yāva kṣaṇa ṭappendu ī ṭoṅge muridarēnu
tatkṣaṇa hāri hōguve – nā
tatkṣaṇa hāri hōguve

Likes, dislikes, hatred, conflicts shall not touch me. I will cultivate a pure heart. The moment the dry twig breaks, that very moment shall I fly away .

kempu sūrya sañjeyalli hakki gūḍu seruvante
ātmadalli ondāguve
bēga bēga pāṭha kaliyuve – nā
tappanella tiddi koḷḷuve

As a bird returning to its nest when the crimson sun sets in the evening, I shall merge in the Self. I shall learn my lessons so I shall correct my mistakes soon.

ānondō ānondō (Bengali)

ānondō ānondō ānondō hai
ōnantō dhōrār mājhē ānondō hai
tumhi aklāntō abhisrāntō aśambhāvō hai
tumhi nīrantō aphūrantō porambrahmō hai

O bliss, bliss! Bliss pervades this eternal universe! You are tireless, never resting, the impossible. You are the endless, ceaseless, supreme Brahman.

tumhi hai śāntō, tumhi aśāntō praḷayōmōyō hai
tumhi hai bhūtō tumhi adbhūtō bhabhiśatō hai
tumhi pracaṇḍō ōkhaṇḍō brahmāṇḍō hai
tumhi ākārō śākārō nirākārō hai

You are calm, and unresting, You are of the form of dissolution. You are the wonderful. You are the past and the future! You are fierce, You are unbroken, You are the Universe! You are both the formless and the one with a form.

tumhi prakāśō tumhi ākāśō jyōtirmōyō hai
tumhi praśārō tumhi ōśārō gōtimōyō hai
onantō brahmāṇḍō mājhē paramō śato hai

koruṇāmōyō dayāmōyō prēmōmōyō hai

You are expanse, You are space, You are full of light. You are progression, You are stillness, You are force. In the eternal Universe, You are the only Truth. You are merciful and, full of kindness. Your very nature is love!

antarātmāvil (Malayalam)

antarātmāvil-ullasiccīṭum
santatānanda-rūpiṇi
hanta! nin-tiru-vaibhavaṅgaḷe
cinta ceyyān-eḷutalla

O embodiment of eternal bliss delighting in the depths my heart! It is impossible to fathom Your greatness, Your sacred glory.

ghōraghōram tapam ceyyunnōrkkum
kaivarunnilla sāyūjyam
'ammē nī mātram' enn-uraykkumbōḷ
vannīṭum janma-sāphalyam

Even those who perform severe penance do not attain liberation. But when we sincerely utter "Mother, only You," our birth is fulfilled.

kālakālanām kāmāri pōlum
kāliṇa tava kūppunnu!
kālattinde karaṅgaḷil-enne
kāḷikē koṭuttīṭolle

Lord Shiva, who defeated even death, worships Your feet. O Kali, please do not give me into the hands of Death!

vāṇi! en manō-vīṇā-tantri nin
gānam ceyyaṭṭe sāmōdam

veṇtinkaḷ-prabha vellum nin mukha-
kānti kaṇḍ-uṇaraṭṭe ñān!

O Goddess Saraswati, may the strings of the veena of my mind sing joyfully to You. May I awaken to the ethereal beauty of Your face, more radiant than the cool, silvery moonlight.

arikil-uṇḍenn-amma (Malayalam)

arikil-uṇḍenn-amma eppōzhum amma tan
maṭiyil-āṇ ī makan ennum-ennum
amṛtattin narumuttam nalki-aṇaykkunna
narunilā-snēham-āṇende amma

My Mother is always close to me. Forever and ever, this child is in Her lap. Showering me with Her kisses of immortality, She embraces me. My Mother is love of the silvery moon.

niravin puñciri-ppūkaḷ pozhiykkum
nirupama-snēha-pravāham amma
karutalāy kanavilum kāttu-ninnīṭunna
karuṇārdra snēham-āṇende amma

In the fullness of Her golden smile, Mother is the incomparable flow of love. She protects us with compassion, even in our dreams. My mother's heart melts with compassion.

cumalile prārabdha-bhāram-ellām – oru
ciriyāl-akattunna puṇyam-amma
caritārtthanāyi ñān maruvunna-nēram-en
ciriyil nin puñciripū viriññu

With one smile, Mother rids us of the burden of our karma. When I live in contentment, Your golden smile blooms through me.

aham-innu pōy-maraññīṭaṭṭe amma nin
alivil-ennum aliññīṭaṭṭe ñān
anutāpa-cintakaḷ nirayum-enn-akatāril
amṛtamāy-amma niraññiṭṭaṭṭe

May I be rid of ego, Mother. May I forever melt in your compassion. May my sorrowful heart be filled with Mother's bliss.

arinda nabarukkō (Tamil)

arinda nabarukkō perumai
ariya seydavarkkō
kattra siruvarukkō perumai
kattru tandavarukkō

Who can be proud: the person who knows or the teacher who taught him? Who can be proud: the learned child or the teacher who taught him?

paḍarnda koṭiyilō perumai
paṭarum marattilō
vaḷarnda marattilō perumai
vaḷarkkum nilattilō
ēndi nirkka onṭrillāmal
eduvum vaḷarumō

Who can be proud: the learned child or the teacher who taught him? What can be proud: the tree or the land it grows on? Can anything grow without a support to hold onto?

paravum maṇattilō perumai
parappum malarilō

viriyum malarilō perumai
virikkum kadirilō
māttramillā onṭrillāmal
māttram nigazhumō

What can be proud: the spreading fragrance or the flower that spreads it? What can be proud: the blooming flower or the sunlight that helps it to bloom? Can change happen without the Unchanging One?

uyarnda nabarukkō perumai
uyara seydavarkkō
uyarvu aruḷai sārndirukka
unnil ahankarippō
guruvin aruḷ illāmal inkē
eduvum naṭakkumō

Who can be proud: the person who reaches great heights in life or the one who helped him? How can one be egoistic when all accomplishments depend on Grace? Can anything happen without the Grace of the Guru?

ārōmal pūmpaitalē (Malayalam)

ārōmal pūmpaitalē kaṇṇā
prēma-nilāvoḷiyē
akatāril-ānandam ēkum nin
prēma manōjña-svarūpam

O darling Krishna, You are tender as a flower. You are like silvery moonbeams of love. Your loving, beautiful form fills my heart with bliss.

tāḷam piṭikkum hṛdantam kaṇṇā
tēṭunnu kāl-taḷamēḷam

maññа-paṭṭuṭayāṭa cārtti kaṇṇā
tiruvuṭal tēja-svarūpam
tiruvuṭal tēja-svarūpam

My heart longs to beat in time to Your tinkling anklets. Yellow silk robes clothe Your radiant form.

ā prēma-tāḷattil-uḷḷam nityam
nṛttam-āṭīṭān kotippū
prēmānantābdhiyil muṅgi kaṇṇā
nityamāy ninnil-aliyān
nityamāy ninnil-aliyān

My heart yearns to dance forever to the rhythm of Your love. Krishna, I long to dive into the ocean of love and bliss and merge in You forever...

ñān tanne nīyenn-ariyān kaṇṇā
ninnil-ennuṇmaye tēṭān
paramātma divya-poruḷē kaṇṇā
ātma-svarūpam-āyīṭān
ātma-svarūpam-āyīṭān

... to know that I am You, Krishna, to find my true Self in You. Krishna, you are the Supreme Self, my divine essence. I long to merge in You, to be of the nature of the Self.

ārtta-bandhuvāya dēvi (Malayalam)

ārtta-bandhuvāya dēvi
cērttaṇaccu conna mantram
tīrttum-ende hṛttaḍattil
vārtteḍuttu mōkṣa cinta

O Mother, the refuge of the distressed, the mantra You whispered as You hugged me close to You awakened in my the desire for spiritual liberation.

kīrttanam ceytīḍuvānāy
ōrtteḍukkān allalilla
kārtyāyani hṛdiyil
nṛtta-nṛtyam-āḍukayāl

I have no difficulty to remember and chant the mantra, O Kartyayani, because You revel in my heart. I sing Your songs of glory with effortless ease, O Kartyayani, as You dance in the depths of my heart.

cērttuvacca putra-vṛndam
hṛttunīri tēngiḍumbōḷ
ārttalakkyum-āzhi tāṇḍi
tīrtthamāy nī vannaṇayum

When Your children cry in distress, You come as the sacred waters, to carry them across the turbulent ocean of transmigration.

kōrttuvacca varṇṇa-māla
cārttuvānāy-orttiḍumbōḷ
tīrttum-ente hṛttaḍattil
mūrttamākum viśva-rūpam

When I dwell in memories of You, yearning to adorn You with the flower garland I wove, Your cosmic form appears in my heart.

aruṇōdayattiṅkal (Malayalam)

aruṇōdayattiṅkal himabindu kaṇḍiṭṭu
paitalō mōhiccu vaiḍhūryamāy

ajñāna-hētuvāl vāsthavam kāṇāññu
martyarō āyussu vyartthamākki

Seeing the dew drop at sunrise, this child mistakes it for a precious gem. Because of their ignorance, human beings waste their lives not seeing the Truth.

ānandam tēṭinām naśvara-bhōgaṅgaḷ
svantam-ākkīṭuvān ōṭiyennāl
ātmāvin sāram-ariyātta jīvanum
vibhramam kāṭṭunna paitaḷallē

Seeking happiness, we run after fleeting pleasures. Aren't we deluded children if we do not know the eternal Self?

kaṇṇatinn-uḷkkāzhcay-ēkuvān īśvaran
kaṇmunnil-ettumbōḷ kāṇākēṇam...
kara-kaḷaññīṭaṇam hṛdaya-śrīkōvilil
kamanīya-rūpam pratiṣṭhikkaṇam

We should recognize God when he comes before us to grant us insight. The temple of our heart should be cleansed, that we may enshrine His beautiful form.

āvō muraḷīdhar (Hindi)

āvō muraḷīdhar mēre pās
āvō muraḷīdhar
muraḷī kē gītōṅ kō tērē
sunnē-kō mē taras rahī kānhā

O Krishna, flute-bearer, do come to me. I wait in agony to hear You play the songs on your flute...

muraḷī bajākē kyā tum
gayāṅ carā rahē hō
yā phir kahīṅ gōpiyōṅ kē
mākhan curā rahē hō
kahāṅ hō...

Are you playing Your flute while the cows graze? Or are You stealing butter from some cowherd girl?

kāhāṅ hō tum jaldi āvō... ō
hē prēm kē sāgar mērē kānhā

Where are You? Come quickly, O Ocean of Love, my darling Krishna!

paṅghaṭ par phirsē naṭkhaṭ
līla tum kar rahē hō
yā phir saṅg gōpiyōṅkē
rās racā rahē hō
kahāṅ hō...

Are You getting ready to enact another drama on the banks of the river? Or are You again dancing the divine rasa with the cowherd girls?

āyēṅgē mērē kānhā āj (Hindi)

āyēṅgē mērē kānhā āj
miṭ jāyēgi naynōṅ ki pyās
murjhāyē is jīvan mēṅ
āyēgi ab phir sē bahār

My Krishna will come today, and quench the thirst of my eyes. Again there will be spring in my wilted life .

āñcal sē vō lag jāyēgā
kahtē huvē... mā... ō... mā...
pūchūṅgi us sē rōtē – hastē
yād kaisē mēri āyi āj

He will cling to me saying, "Mother, O mother." With laughter and tears, I will ask Him, "How is it that you remembered me today?"

vādā usē karnā hōgā
chōḍ na jāyēgā mā kō kabhi
hōkē judā nandalālā sē
rah na sakūṅgi ik pal bhī

He will have to promise never again to leave mother. Separated from little Krishna, I cannot bear to live for even a moment.

kānhā... kānhā...
kānhā... kānhā...

āyōrē āyōrē kānhā (Hindi)

āyōrē āyōrē kānhā sakhāvōṅ kē saṅg
vṛndāvan kē sundar vanōṅ mēṅ
mauj mēṅ bitānē sārā hi din
aur naṭkhaṭ līlāyēṅ karnē

Here comes Krishna along with His friends, to the beautiful forests of Vrindavan, to spend the whole day in fun and frolic and do mischievous divine plays.

gōpāl gōpālā rādhē rādhē gōpālā
gōpāl gōpālā rādhē śyām gōpālā

O Krishna, beloved of Radha!

āge āge kānhā caltē calē
pīchē dauḍē gāyēṅ gvāl sārē
vṛndāvan kī kuñj galiyōṅ sē
kānhā kī ṭoli baḍtī gayī

As Krishna walked, all the cowherd boys and girls ran behind. The troupe kept advancing through the narrow lanes of Vrindavan.

cupkē cupkē kānhā cōr kī bhānti
vraj gōpiyōṅ kē ghar ghus jātē
dahi miśari mākhan kē saṅg
unkē dil bhī kanhā curā lētē

Quietly, like a thief, Krishna crept into the cowherds' homes. And along with curd and sugar candy, He would steal their hearts too!

nācē nācē kānhā sabkō behlāyē
muraḷi bajākē vō sabkō lubhāyē
apnē tan man aur jag bhūlkē
sārē us dhun mēṅ khō jāyē

Krishna's dancing made everyone rejoice. With His flute playing, He ensnares all. Forgetting body, mind and world, all are lost in that melodious tune.

bahū divasāñcī (Marāṭhi)

bahū divasāñcī manīṣā mājhī āja jhālī purī
māya māulī malā bhēṭalī mātā jagadīśvarī

For long, I've wanted to meet my dear Mother. Now I've met the Mother of the Universe and that wish is fulfilled.

bhaktānsāṭhī prēmasvarūpiṇī kitī ga rūpē ghēśī
kadhī kālikā kadhī lakṣumī kadhī śāradā hōśī
yōgakṣēma pāhī bhaktāñcē mātā bhāgya vidhātrī
māya māulī malā bhēṭalī mātā hṛdayēśvarī

O embodiment of love, how many forms You take for the sake of your devotees! You appear as Kali, Lakshmi and Sharada. O One who bestows good fortune, You care for your devotees' welfare. I met the Mother of my heart!

nakō dēūs antara ṭhēvi nirantara tujhiyā caraṇāsī

Please do not keep me away! Always keep me at your feet.

asthira vyākuḷa mana hē mājhē cañcala hōtē kitī
tulā pāhatā maja na kaḷalē sthirāvalē tē kadhī
dhāvata yēunī mātē majalā hṛdayājavaḷī dharī
māya māulī malā bhēṭalī mātā paramēśvarī

After your darshan my unsteady, agitated, wavering mind became calm and peaceful. O Mother, please hold me close to You. I met the Supreme Mother!

tujhyā śīvāya mājhē śāśvata asē kharē ga kōṇa
asēna tēthuni dhāvō mājhē tujhiyā pāyī mana
kṛpādṛṣṭī tū ṭhēva nirantara āmhā bhaktānvarī
māya māulī malā bhēṭalī mātā śivaśankarī

O Mother, please hold me close. I met the Supreme Mother! May you always look benevolently on your devotees. I met Goddess Parvati (consort of Lord Shiva)!

bandu chē (Gujarati)

bandu chē mā hṛdayanā dvār
khōlō mā tamē kṛpā nidhān
ajñānamā khūpī rahyō āj
kṛpā karō hē kṛpānidhān

Mother, the door of my heart is closed. O treasure of compassion, please open it for me. I am sinking in the dirt of ignorance. O treasure of grace, please shower your Grace!

manmā mārā cōr tē pāñc
kām krōdh mad lōbh mōh
mannē lūṭē din nē rāt
rakṣā karō hē rakṣaṇahār

The five thieves of lust, anger, pride, greed and delusion attack me day and night. Mother, save me.

ahamnō lāgyō rōg manē kēvō
layi jāy manē jāṇē kyā
āvāna mēdanē tāri pās
tārā sivā manē kōni ās

The disease of ego eats me up and drags me in every direction. It keeps me from reaching Your side. What refuge do I have other than You?

sācu ēk nām mānu bāki kēvanā
nām bhajilē mānu tāri sāthē haśē sadā

Mother, Your name is the only Truth. All other names are mere names. Chant Mother's name. Only that will always remain with us.

bhagavān kahāṅ (Hindi)

bhagavān kahāṅ bhagavān kahāṅ,
ḍhūṇḍā usē yahāṅ vahāṅ

Where is God, O where is He? I have searched here and there.

mandir mēṅ masjid mēṅ
tīrath mēṅ ōr mūrat mēṅ
himālay kī ēkānt mēṅ
niścal man kē maun mēṅ
bhagavān kahāṅ bhagavān kahāṅ,
ḍhūṇḍā usē yahāṅ vahāṅ

I have looked in temples, in mosques, in pilgrimages, in idols, in the silent Himalayas, in the quiet of my still heart. Where is God, O where is He? I have searched here and there.

dhyān kiyā bhajan kiyā
sukh ōr bhōg kā tyāg kiyā
sēvā bhāv sē dān kiyā
śāstr granth kā manan kiyā
bhagavān kahāṅ bhagavān kahāṅ,
ḍhūṇḍā usē yahāṅ vahāṅ

I meditated and sang His glories, renounced happiness and pleasures. I did charity with a selfless attitude, and studied the scriptures. Where is God, O where is He? I have searched here and there.

bhaṭak bhaṭak kē pāyā khud kō
sadguru caraṇ chāyā mēṅ
pūchā mainē bhagavān kahāṅ
guru batlāyē tū hī bhagavān

jhāṅk bhītar pehechān khud kō
sākṣāt-kar apnē param pad kō
phir... bhagavān yahāṅ bhagavān vahāṅ
jahāṅ dēkhē bhagavān vahāṅ

I asked my Guru "Where is God?" and my Guru said, "You Are God."
I asked my Guru "Where is God?" And the Guru said, "You Are God."
No matter where you look, the Lord is there.

mandir mēṅ bhagavān, masjid mēṅ bhagavān
tīrath mūrat rūp-rūp mēṅ, ab dikh tē bhagavān
dhyān mēṅ bhagavān, bhajan mēṅ bhagavān
maun vācc śabd śabd mēṅ gūñjtē bhagavān
sukh mēṅ bhagavān dukh mēṅ bhagavān
hastē rōtē bhāv bhāv kē dhartā hai bhagavān
tan mēṅ bhagavān man mēṅ bhagavān
jag kē kaṇ kaṇ mēṅ rahate haiṅ bhagavān

God is in the temple, God is in the mosque. In pilgrimage, in idols, in all forms is God. Now I see God. God in meditation, God in singing. In silence, in speech, in every word, is God. In happiness is God, in sorrow is God. In laughter, in tears, in every emotion is God. In the body is God, in the mind is God. In every atom of the Universe is God, just God.

tan mēṅ bhagavān
man mēṅ bhagavān

In the body is God, in the mind is God.

bhajlē rām rām rām (Hindi)

bhajlē rām rām rām, sitā rām
bhajlē rām rām rām, sitā rām

janam tērā, saphal karēṅgē rām

Sing Ram Ram Sita Ram, and He will make your life worthwhile.

śabarī kē jaisā, bhāv jagāle
nirmal apnē, man kō banāle
man kī kuṭiyā, kō tū sajālē
rām nām kē dīp jalāle
khud āyēṅgē rām
janam tērā, saphal karēṅgē rām

Make your heart like Shabari's (the great humble devotee of Rama). Make it pure and thus decorate the hut of your heart (like Shabari's hut). Light the lamp of the name of Rama and He will come to you. He will make your life worthwhile.

viṣayōṅ sē tū, man kō haṭālē
har ik sāṅs mē rām basālē
rām dikhēṅgē, antar man mē
andar bāhar, har ik kaṇ mē
cārōṅ or haiṅ rām
janam tērā, saphal karēṅgē rām

Leave the distractions of life and let the Lord reside in your every breath. Then you will see Rama in your inner abode. Inside and outside, in every atom, in all the four directions is Ram. He will make your life worthwhile.

rām ōr brahm, alag-alag nahīṅ
rām saguṇ hai, ōr nirguṇ bhī
kōyi bulāyē, rām prabhū jī
sītā pati bhī, puruṣōttam bhī
rām kē hī sab nām

janam tērā, saphal karēṅgē rām

Rama is not different from Brahma. Rama exists with and without attributes. Some may call him Lord Rama, or some as the husband of Sita, and some as the Supreme Being. All are the names of the One supreme. He will make your life worthwhile.

bhakti dē mā (Hindi)

bhakti dē mā bhakti dē mā
dē mā bhakti bhakti dē mā
bhakti dē mā bhakti dē mā
ik varadān maiṅ tujhsē māṅgū
prēm bhakti tū dēnā mā
prēm bhakti tū dēnā mā

Bless me with devotion, Divine Mother, bless me with devotion! Devotion is the only blessing that I seek from You, Mother. The highest form of love!

mōh rāg sab dūr karō mā
cain tū man kā dēnā mā
divya prēm sē mujhkō bhar dē
man nirmal kar dē mā – mērā
man nirmal kar dē

O Mother, annihilate all attachments and passions from my mind. Thereby grant me peace. Fill me with divine love, O Mother, that my mind may be purified. Make my mind pure, O Mother!

dvār tērē maiṅ āyā hūṅ maiyā
śaraṇ mēṅ mujhkō lē lō mā
man kō apnā bandhī banā lō

tum mēṅ līn rahē mā – bas
tum mēṅ līn rahē mā

My Mother, I come to Your doorstep; please give me refuge! Please make my mind Your prisoner, that it may ever be merged in You.

tav caraṇōṅ mēṅ āyā maiyā
mujhkō tū apnā lē
bhakti kā vardān dē mujhē
apnē mēṅ hi samā lē

Dear Mother, now that I have reached Your lotus feet, please accept me as Your own. Please grant me the boon of devotion and absorb me in You!

birahō āgune (Bengali)

birahō āgune jōlichē hṛdōy
bōlītē nārī tōrē bidāy
mā hōyē mōrē, bhūlē gēlī
kālī tū hōlī mṛṇmayi

My heart aches in the fire of separation. I can't say 'goodbye' to You. O Mother, You forgot me. O Kali, You became a frozen statue.

kāḷī mā kāḷī mā kāḷī mā kāḷī mā
kāḷī mā kāḷī mā kāḷī mā kāḷī mā
bhēbē dākh mā tuyi nije
jōgōt bhūlē ēlō tōr kāchē
jōgōt bhūlē ēlō tōr kāchē
tōr-nōyōne-śubhi nijere bhūle
tāu ki nibinā kōlē tule

O Mother, please reflect: Leaving everything behind I came to you. I will sleep under your watchful gaze. Will you still not take me in Your lap?

hāriye kōtō dikēr mājhē
pāgōḷ hōlam tōke khuje
pāgōḷ hōlam tōke khuje
ar kōrō na dērī ōmā
lōkhi hōyē nāu mākōlē

I am getting lost in all directions and have become mad searching for You. Please don't wait any longer. Please be a good mother and take me in Your lap.

bōlo śyām rādhē rādhē (Hindi)

vandē nanda vṛjastrīṇām pādarēṇum
abhīkṣṇaśaha
yāsām harikathōtgītam punāti bhuvana-trayam

I bow to the dust at the feet of the women of Vraj (Krishna's birthplace), whose song of Lord Hari purifies the three worlds.

bōlo śyām rādhē rādhē, rādhē rādhē syām
bhav sāgar kō pār karāye śyāmji kā nām

Sing "Radhe Shyam!" The name of Krishna will carry you across the ocean of samsara.

vṛndāvan mathurā nahīṅ kēval unkā dhām
bhaktōṅ kē hṛdayōn mēṅ vō kartē haiṅ viśrām
bhūkhe haiṅ bas bhāvē kō bhāv hō niṣkām
dil sē pukārō āyēṅgē vō prabhu dayānidhān
prēm se bhajlē ab tu manvā rādhē rādhē śyām

He resides not only in Vrindavan or Mathura. He is found in the hearts of his devotees. All he looks for is selfless love. Call him from your inner heart and the compassionate Lord will come. Chant the name of Radhe Shyam with love.

sūr mīrā sab nē pāyā ānand kā dhām
lēnā kabhi na bhūlē vō giridhāri kā nām
un caraṇōṅ kō pāyē binā na karanā tu ārām
dhanya banā dē apnā jīvan bhajlē rādhē śyām
prēm se bhajlē ab tu manvā rādhē rādhē śyām

Saints like Surdas and Mira all reached the highest bliss. They remembered always to chant the name of the Lord. Do not waste your time and miss reaching those divine feet. Make your life worthwhile by chanting Radhe Shyam. Chant the name Radhe Shyam with love!

cēsēdi nīvamma (Telugu)

cēsēdi nīvamma ceppukonēdi mēmamma
idi ēmi ñāyamamma (2)

O Mother, though You do all the work, we take credit for it. Why is that?

sūryuni veligiñcitivamma
candruniki śōbhaniccitivamma
viśvamunē sṛṣṭiñcitivamma
māku garvamu ēla icitivamma?

You endow the sun with light and energy. You lend beauty to the moon. You created the whole universe. Why then did You make us so proud?

paramēśvari bhuvanēśvari
jagadīśvari śaraṇam śaraṇam

O Supreme Goddess, Goddess of the Earth, Goddess of the World, grant us refuge!

aviṭṭini koṇḍalu ekkiñcitivamma
mūganu mahākavini cēsitivamma
mā buddhini naḍipēdi nīvē amma
'nēnu cēsitinanna' aham nadamma

By Your grace, the lame can scale mountains, and the mute can wax lyrical. It is You who illumine the intellect. Why have You allowed the sense of doer-ship in us?

chod de mānase (Odiya version)

chāḍi dē manaru duḥkha ra cintā
sumaraṇa kara ēī satya rē
dēha nohu tuhī mana bī nohū tū
kebaḷa ātmā tū jāṇīnē

hārī galū tūhī sukha khojī
khojī duniyāra sabū bhōgare
paramānanda jē tōharī antarē
tharē tahinki tū cāhānrē

mora tora ēī bhēdabhāba nēī
sānti bhalā kāhūn pāyibū
sabūrī bhītarē ēkayi ātmā
tū hī sabū ṭhārē vyāpta rē

ātmāra rāija tōrī āpaṇāra rē
mana tū kēbē nohū dīna

parama santira jhara to bhītare
re mana tū kebe nohū hīna

cinmay sundar (Marathi)

cinmay sundar mūrti sājirī
gaṇēś āvāhan man mandirī
manōbhāvē karu mānas pūjā
āratī ovāḷū gaṇarājā...

Lord Ganesh of blissful, beautiful form, I invite You into the temple of my heart. Worshiping You sincerely, I perform Arati to You (traditional sacred showing of flame).

gaṇapati bāppā gaṇapati bāppā gaṇapati bāppa mōrayā
maṅgaḷa-mūrti maṅgaḷa-mūrti maṅgaḷa-mūrti mōrayā

Lord Ganesh, auspicious One, victory to You!

varad-hasta bhakt kaivārī
gaurī-nandan vighna nivārī
śudh manācā naivēdya dākhavū
sadā sarvadā tulā āṭhavū

Son of Parvati, remover of obstacles, You are ever ready to bless your devotees. I lay before You the offering of a pure heart. May I always behold You everywhere.

gaṇarāyālā bhāvē vanduni
cittavṛtti caraṇī arpuni
ēkāgr hō-u nāma-smaraṇī

bhakti-bhāva jāgavū manī

I bow to Lord Ganesha, offering mind and heart at His holy feet. May I chant your holy name with single-minded focus, and thus awaken true devotion in my heart.

nitya ghaḍū dē tujhē cintan
bharunī rāhō pūrṇ samādhān
hṛdayī dēvā mantr rūpē rahā
gam gaṇapatayē namō namaḥ

Contemplating You constantly, may I always remain content. Stay in my heart in the form of the great mantra: "gam ganapataye namo namah."

citaykkarikil (Malayalam)

citaykk-arikil vitumbi-nilkkum
svajana-bandhaṅgaḷ pakṣē
atu-kazhiññāl mizhi-tuṭaccavar
akannu-pōyīṭum

Our near and dear ones will sob beside the funeral pyre. Then they will wipe away their tears and walk away.

mṛtippeṭillann-uraccu svapnam
menaññu-kuṭṭunnu ellām
viphalam-ākum nizhalu-pōl yaman
arikil nilkkunnu

We entertain grand dreams, forgetting that death will come for us. But such dreams fail to materialize. The God of Death stalks us like our own shadow.

kaṇakkutāḷil kuriccu-veccoru

dinam aṇayumbōḷ ārkkum
uṭu-tuṇikk-oru-maru-tuṇikkum
samayam-ēkilla

When the preordained time of our death arrives, we will not even have time to change our clothes!

paṭi-kaṭannā-yaman-aṇaññāl
marañň-irunnīṭān svantam
uṭalu-pōlum iṭam tarill-aviṭat-
-azhiññu vīṇiṭum

When the God of Death crosses the threshold, we won't even be able to hide behind our body. It will fall away from the Self.

uyirum-ūṭalum vērpiriññāl
uyiru-śēṣikkum vīṇḍum
uṭalināyi pala kaṭambakaḷ
kaṭannu-pōrēṇam

When the Self and body are separated, the Self alone remains. It must overcome many obstacles before attaining a new body.

svayam ariññ-avan ariyum eṅgane
mṛtiye-vennīṭām – ennām
jananam ennatu maraṇam ennatu
phalita-vākyaṅgaḷ

One who knows his own Self can conquer death. When man has realized his Self, he can smile at the words 'birth' and 'death'.

dē darśan mā (Odiya version)

dē darśana mā dēbī mā ambē mā bhabānī mā

bandhu parijana bandhana micchā
mā sata ēkā sinā sēnēha tōra
dhana jana māna sabu micchā mā gō
sata ekā khālī prēma tōra

jai jai mā jai jai mā
jai jai mā jai jai mā

ē bhaba sāgara pāri kara mōtē
dhanya kari dē mā jībana mōrā
abōdha sīsu mu nīya kōḷē mā go
jagão antarē parama prēma

Desire leads to anger (English)

Desire leads to anger,
from anger follows fear.
The door opens for hatred
and sorrow's coming near.

Take my shame, take my pride,
everything, deep inside.
I need you. I'm hopeless
without your grace.

I surrender my mistakes.

surrendering desire...
opening to grace...
a love that has no limits...

In your tender embrace,
accepting all and serving,
peace and joy come near.
Self-confidence gives courage,
and faith replaces fear.

dil kō banā dō (Hindi)

dil kō banā dō madhuban
jahāṅ nācē kānhā rādhā saṅg
man kō banā dō vṛndāvan
jahāṅ basē kānhā har ik kṣaṇ
kānhā rē ō... kānhā rē...
hamnē sauṅpā tujhē
apnā tan man

Make your heart the playground where the Lord Krishna dances with Radha. Make your heart the abode where Krishna resides every moment. O Krishna. I surrender my body and heart to You.

rāt divas yahāṅ līlā racāvō
man mandir kō nivās banāvō
nayan mūndē tujhē bhītar pāvūṅ
har pal dil mēṅ rās racāvūṅ
kānhā rē ō... kānhā rē...
tujhkō hī pāvūṅ pās har – ik kṣaṇ

Make the temple of my heart Your home. There You can enact Your Divine play day and night. Whenever I close my eyes, may I behold You. O Krishna, may I dance with You and find only You every single moment.

prēm bharī nazrōṅ sē nihārō
pyār bharī muskān luṭāvō
bāṅsurī kī ik madhur tān sē
ānand sāgar mēṅ lē jāvō
kānhā rē ō... kānhā rē...
hamnē kiyā tujhē jīvan arpaṇ

Look upon me with love-filled eyes, O Lord. Cast upon me Your love-filled smile. With one sweet note of Your flute, immerse me in the ocean of bliss. O Krishna, I surrender this life to You.

Don't let me waste this life (English)

Don't let me waste this life,
don't let me waste this life.

Senses run wild,
attachments have piled
upon your darling child.

By a touch from you I have come,
choosing a life doubted by some,
to live by your word
that in silence is heard
with hopes this 'I' will be cured.

Now at your feet I try
to realize before I die

the Truth that you know,
the compassion you show,
may love forever grow.

By serving you I'll be free.
Your presence in humanity,
for You are in me
and all that I see—
this opportunity.

ē amma! (Telugu)

ē amma! mūḍu jagamulanu ēlēṭṭiyamma
ē amma! muggurammalaku mūlapuṭṭamma
ē amma! sarvāntaryāmiyai uṇḍēṭṭiyamma
ā ammanē... manatō naḍici mananu naḍipiñcu
jagadīśvarī... sarvēśvarī... śrī mātā laḷitā
paramēśvari

The divine mother rules over the three worlds. She is the mother of the three goddesses (Lakshmi, Durga and Saraswati). The divine mother resides within all as their inner Self. The same divine mother walks with us and makes us tread the spiritual path. O Goddess of the world, Goddess of all, divine Mother Lalita, supreme Goddess!

sarva lōkamulaku śānti
sarva jīvamulaku śānti
sarva svarūpiṇī jayahō
sarva śaktimayī jayahō
jayahō... jayahō... jayahō...

May all worlds be peaceful, may all beings be peaceful. Victory to the divine mother, who is the embodiment of all forms. Victory to divine mother, who is the embodiment of all energies. Victory to divine mother!

ē amma! manatōḍugā nilaci mananu
rakṣiñcēṭṭiyamma
ē amma! manalōnēvuṇḍi mananu śāśin
cēṭṭiyamma
ē amma! manatō jīviñci manaku guruvai
nilicinayamma
ā ammanē... manatō naḍici, mananu naḍipiñcu
jagadīśvarī... sarvēśvarī... śrī mātā laḷitā
paramēśvari

The divine mother stands with us and protects us. She dwells within us and rules us. The divine mother has become our Guru and lives with us. O Goddess of the world, Goddess of all, divine Mother Lalita, supreme Goddess!

sarva lōkamulaku śānti
sarva jīvamulaku śānti
śānti pradāyini jayahō
śaraṇa dāyini jayahō
jayahō... jayahō... jayahō...

May all worlds be peaceful, may all beings be peaceful. Victory to the divine Mother who bestows peace and refuge. Victory to You!

ē duniyā hai (Punjabi)

ē duniyā hai nirā tamāśā

ē cār dinōṅ dā hai vāsā
kadī rōṇā tē kadī hāṅsā
kadī āśā tē kadī nirāśā

This world is entirely a play, a place of temporary existence. With some tears and some laughter, at times we have hope and at other times despair.

nā duḥkh raine nā sukh raine
nā bhain bharā mā pē raine
ē tan gaine kujj nayī raine
terē nāmō-niśā nā kōī raine
gurucaraṇ caraṇ lē śaraṇ śaraṇ
ē duniyā hai nirā tamāśā

Sorrow doesn't remain, nor does happiness. Nor will your near and dear ones remain. Neither this body nor wealth, nor trace of your name and fame will remain.

sab apnē nē nā kōī bagānā
kujj lēkē nayī aithō jāṇā
hūṇ chaḍh dē tū mēmē karnā
pachtāyēṅgā nayī tā varnā
gurucaraṇ caraṇ lē śaraṇ śaraṇ

Everyone is yours, no one is separate. From here you can take nothing as your own. At least now stop saying 'me and mine,' or else you will have to repent. Take refuge at the feet of your Guru.

ēk dīp jalāyē ham (Hindi)

ēk dīp jalāyē ham pyār kā
ēk dīp jalāyē ham viśvās kā

lēkē calē ham yē jyōt sārē jag mēṅ
phailāyē ham sandēś śānti kā

Let us light a lamp of love, let us light a lamp of faith. Let us take this light all over the world and spread the message of peace.

ōm lōkāḥ samastāḥ sukhinō bhavantu

May all the beings in all the worlds be happy.

muskān sē bharā hō har cehrā
miṭ jāyē jag sē ātaṅk kā andhērā
jiyē sukh ōr śānti sē jan sārē
khudā kardō yē sapnā sacc hamārā

Let a smile light up every face, let the darkness of terrorism disappear from the world. Let all people live in happiness and peace. O Lord, fulfill our dream!

miṭ jāyē yē mānavi sīmāyēṅ
mansē man har insān kā juḍ jāyē
zarūrat mandoṅ kī karē sēvā
ismē pāyē ham tuṣṭi hamēśā

Let man-made boundaries vanish. Let the minds of everyone unite. Let us serve the needy and find contentment and happiness forever.

banāyē ham milke nayā daur
kadam sē kadam baḍhāyēṅ iskī ōr
bin kōyī santāp aur śōk
jiyē is jag mēṅ sab lōg

Let us create a new era together. Let us walk together toward this goal. Let all the people live in this world free of all feelings of anguish and grief.

ēk vacani ēk bāṇi (Marathi)

ēk vacani ēk bāṇi asā mājhyā rāmrāyā
hē raghunandan kuḷōddhāri var dē āhmā guṇgāyā

The one of truthful word is my Ramaraya. O Lord of the Raghu clan, upholder of the kula. Our Savior of clans, we thank you,

avatarḷā yajñi putrkāmēṣṭi
daśarath kuḷi avadhpuri
kōmaḷ śyāmaḷ rājīv-nētri
asur bhañjak dhanurdhāri
mātṛpitṛ ājñāpālak nighē
vanā jāyā hē raghuvamśī

You incarnated out of Putrkameshthi Yajna in the clan of Dasharata in Ayodhya. Your tender body is dark, and your eyes are like lotus petals. You hold the bow and slay the evil (demons); obeying Your parents, You left for the forest, O Lord Raghuvanshi!

uddharisi tū jaḍ jīvānā
caitanya mati bhakti dēsi
ṛṣī muniyāñcē yāg rakṣisi
sṛṣṭi śānti sṛjan kari
bhārmukt kari dharaṇimātā
sakaḷā śānti ānandā

O Savior of souls in bondage, grant me enlightened intellect and devotion. You protect the sacrificial rites of the rishis. Protector of subjects, you are the giver of happiness

prajā-pālakā sukh-pradāyakā
bhakta-vatsal dīnōddhāri

rām rājā amar bhūvarī
ādarś hōyi mānav jagati
dīpastambh tamhāri tū
nītimay hē avatāri

Affectionate to the devotees, you free the downtrodden. You are King Rama, immortal on Earth. You are an ideal for mankind, a lighthouse and absolver of tamas, an example of morality.

raghupati rāghava rājārām patita pāvana sītārām

Victory to Rama, lord of the Raghus, uplifter of the down-trodden, Sita Rama!

entinu śokam (Telugu version)

ēla ī śōkam manasā
nī nija bhāvamadi kādu
sāndra sukhāmṛta sāmrajyamlō
ēkādhipati ani erugu

mārppu anunadi mārani niyamam
mārani vastuvani gurttiñcu
maru bhūmilō eṇḍamāvula pōle
māyākṛtamī jagamantā

āndhyam tyajiñcu manasā akhilamu
ātmēyani grahiyiñcu
erukana śrīmukha prabha darśiñcu
erigetḍu ahamē nī rūpam

Eons of lifetimes (English)

Eons of lifetimes
seeking the divine,
I wake to your drum
and call out śivoham!

So long I am seeking
freedom from samsāra.
My heart keeps repeating
om namah śivaya
om namah śivaya, om namah śivaya
My heart keeps repeating om namah śivaya

Stuck in the vast mires
of fears and desires,
I wake to your drum
and call out shivoham!

gaṇēśa namaḥ ōm (Odiya version)

gaṇēśa namaḥ ōm
gaṇēśa namaḥ ōm
gaṇēśa namaḥ śrī
gaṇēśa namaḥ ōm

hē gaṇanāyaka śubhaphaladāyaka
bighna-bināsanakārī
bidyādāyaka buddhipradāyaka

siddhibināyaka swāmī

tōrī pūjā karē bhakata pahilē
gāē sē tōrī mahimā
dura kara prabhu sabu amaṅgala
sukha rē bharu ē duniyāṅ

gaṇēśa siddhi dātā (Hindi)

gaṇēśa siddhi dātā
mahēś kē kumārā
samasta vighna nāśā
namō bhavāniputrā

Ganesh! giver of divine powers, son of Shiva. We bow before you, destroyer of obstacles, son of Goddess Parvati.

jay gaṇēś... jay gaṇēś...
jay gaṇēś... jay gaṇēś...
jay gaṇēś jay gaṇēś jay gaṇēś jay
jay gaṇēśa jay... jay gaṇēśa jay...

Victory to Ganesh!

tum hī karōgē mangal
samasta vighna bhañjan
bhajē tumāri mūrat
karō hamārā rañjan

Bestower of auspiciousness, destroyer of obstacles. Delight our hearts as we chant your name.

trilōk vāsiyōṅ par

abādh tērā śāsan
tumhārē kōyi pūjak
kabhī na hōtē śrīhīn

O Ruler of the three worlds, no devotee of Yours is ever deprived of auspiciousness.

giri vana puri (Kannada)

girivanapuri tīrtthādigaḷalli
dikku deseyillade alediruve
kanasina māyā lōkada teradi
bhramita manadi nī aledāḍiruvē

You roam aimlessly among mountains, forests, cities and pilgrim centers. You wander in this dream- like world as if you are sleep-walking.

kṛṣi illada bañjaru bhūmi
vivēkavillada ninnāvasthe
manaḥśuddhiyindale jñānodayavu
jñānadindalē śāśvata sukhavu
manujā... manujā... hiḍi nī gurupādā
bēgane kaḷevanu bhava bhārā

Your condition devoid of discernment is like an arid and barren land. Knowledge dawns only in a pure mind. Knowledge bestows lasting happiness. O man, hold on to the Guru's feet. He will remove the burden of worldliness.

vyāghrage sikka jiṅkēya teradi
āgihe nīnu māyāvaṣadi
jīvita vyartthavu āgade irali

aritukō parama tattvava javadi
manujā... manujā... hiḍi nī gurupādā
bēgane kaḷevanu bhava bhārā

Like a deer trapped in a tiger's mouth, maya (cosmic illusion) ensnares you. Quickly realize the ultimate truth, so you don't waste the rest of your life. O man, hold onto the Guru's feet. He will remove the burden of worldliness.

gōkulanāthā gōpakumārā (Tamil)

gōkulanāthā gōpakumārā, gōvindā hari gōvindā
ālilai kaṇṇā āzhiyin vaṇṇā
āṭiṭuvāy en agantanilē

Lord of Gokula, young cowherd boy, Govinda, Hari! O Krishna, You floated on a banyan leaf. Your complexion is like the ocean. Please dance in my heart!

vṛndāvanattin tenṭralumē
un kathai yāvum kūriṭumē
pēsum kiḷiyum vandu enniṭattil
pērazhagan unnai varṇṇikkumē
nittam nittam undan ninaivinilē
cittam siragaṭittu parandiṭumē
nēsam tavira neñcil ēdumillai
ninaiyanṭri enakkinku evarumillai

O Krishna, the breeze of Vrindavan tells your stories. A singing parrot described your beauty to me. Every day my mind soars like a bird in thoughts of You. I have nothing but love in my heart. There is no one for me, except You.

un kuzhal nādam kēṭkaiyilē
en manappūvam pūttiṭumē
nādam vanda disaiyinil ōṭi
nādanin tāḷ vandu sērndiṭumē
suṭṭri suṭṭri vandu unnaṭiyai
pattri paṭarum oru pūnkoṭi nān
sōgam ēdumillai un ninaivāl
sukham tarum maṇamē en manadil

O Krishna, my heart blossoms when I hear Your flute music. Running toward Your music, I reach Your holy feet. I am a vine encircling Your holy feet in order to grow. Memories of You erase all my sadness leaving only Your sweet fragrance.

gōkulanāthā gōvindā – gōpakumārā gōvindā
gōvindā hari gōvindā gōvindā hari gōvindā

gōpālak bāsurī (Hindi)

gōpālak bāsurī sē jab
āyā ēk mōhan gānā
gōlōk mēṅ phailī tab hī
māyā – muraḷī kī jādū

When a beautiful song emerged from Krishna's flute, the magic of Maya (the Grand Illusion) spread in Goloka.

kṛṣṇa kṛṣṇa ghanaśyāma
vēṇugāna rasalōlā
vāsudēva vanamāli
gōkulēś giridhāri

O Krishna, Delighter of Hearts, O Vasudeva, Giridhari, You remove the burdens of Your devotees.

bōlē sab gōkul vāsī
'rādhē śyām kuñj bihārī
gōpījan vallabh pyārē
kālindi tīr bihārī'

All the people of Gokula chant "Radhe Shyam," the Beloved of the Gopis who lived by the river Kalindi.

tārōṅ nē tāl milāyā
barasāyē phūl surōṅ nē
āyī sab gōp vadhū jan
nācī harisē mil sārī

The stars provided the rhythm and the melodies showered flowers. All the Gopis came as brides to dance with their enchanting Lord.

muskāyē madhuban kē phūl
phailī sab aur sugandhi
laharāyī cāndani – sindhu
kānhā kī mahimā gāyī

The flowers smiled and spread their fragrance. The moonlight enveloped all while the oceans sang the glory of Krishna.

hōli āyi khuśiyāṅ (Hindi)

hōli āyi khuśiyāṅ lāyi
hōli kā tyōhār āj āyā hai
prēm kā sandēsā sāth lāyā hai

The festival of Holi has come bringing with it the message of love.

raṅg ḍālne āyē kānhā
gōp gōpiyōṅ nē nahīṅ mānā
āj tō maiṅ raṅg ke rahūṅgā
kānhā nē bhī phir ṭhānā
kānhā nē nikāli baḍi pichkāri
gōp gōpiyōṅ pē paḍ gaye bhārī
gōp gōpī huē sab daṅg
andar bāhar raṅg
kānhā ke raṅg sē
raṅg gayē sārē

When Krishna came to splash the gopis with color, they refused. But the Lord seized His colors and drenched the gopis. They were astonished to find themselves covered in the hues of Krishna.

ab tō rādhā jī nē ṭhānā
nahīṅ chōḍēṅgē tujhē kānhā
aisā raṅgēṅgē tujhkō
nahīṅ bhūlēgā tū raṅgānā
pichkāriyoṅ ko lē apnē saṅg
chup chup lāyī hāthōṅ mēṅ raṅg
kānhā kō prēm sē raṅg ḍālā
pīlā nīlā aur gulābī
prēm sē raṅg ḍālā
hōli kā tyōhār āj

Now Radha decided she would not spare her Lord. "Now we will splash You with color and You will never forget!" Hiding the colors, she saturated Krishna with all her love until he was yellow, blue and rosy. Thus, till today, the festival of Holi is colored with divine love.

hṛdayam dravicc-ozhukum (Malayalam)

hṛdayam dravicc-ozhukum cuṭu
mizhinīr-alayaniśam
janani tava kazhal-tāraṭi
tazhukunn-anu nimiṣam

O Mother! the burning tears from my grieving heart constantly bathe Your lotus feet.

kadanam tiṅgi hṛdayam viṅgi
vadanam maṅgi – iniyum
arutē tava viraham, mama
hṛdayam nīriy-eriyum

My heart is sorrowful and yearns with intense longing for You. My face has lost its luster. I can no longer bear the pain of separation from You.

muzhuveṇmati-dyuti pōl hṛdi
ozhukīṭuka sadayam
āzhalāttuka jagadīśvari
kazhal-tāraṭi tozhunnēn

May You glow in my heart forever with the radiant brightness of the silvery full moon. O Goddess of the world, please remove my sorrow! I pray with folded palms at Your lotus feet.

jana-kōṭikaḷuṭe hṛdaya-ārādhanam
satatam tava pada-malaraṭikaḷ
paramānanda payōdhi-samānam
tava-karuṇāmṛta hṛdayam
janani... janani...

tava karuṇāmṛta hṛdayam

Millions adore Your lotus feet in their hearts. Your compassionate heart is an ocean of supreme bliss.

hṛdinivāsi (Kannada)

hṛdinivāsi hṛṣīkēśa hāṭakāmbaranē
hāḍi hogaḷi ninna mahimē nāvu nalivevu

O indweller of the heart, O Hrishikesha (One with perfect control over the senses, another name for Lord Krishna), clad in golden robes! We sing Your glories and enjoy immense happiness!

gajēndrana bhaktigolidu dhruvana tapake maṇidu
dūrvāsara śāpadinda kāydē ambarīśana
bhūsurēndra ninna bhajise bhayavēkē namage
dhyāna niṣṭhe bhakti nīḍu dāmōdarā

You appreciated the devotion of Gajendra (king of elephants) and the austerity of Dhruva. You protected Ambarisha from Durvasa's curse. O supreme among gods, we have no fear, for we chant Your name. O Damodara (name of Lord Krishna), please bestow on us one-pointed devotion.

gōkula kṛṣṇa gōvinda kṛṣṇa (2)
gōpi-priya kṛṣṇa

Victory to the Lord of the cowherd boys and the Vedas, the beloved of the milk maidens and cows!

kunti-dēvi kai mugiyē pāṇḍavara sakhanāgi
hagaliruḷu kāvaliṭṭu pālisi pōṣiside
bhakta prahlādana bhāvapūrṇa bhaktigē
mecci maguva kaṣṭake sadā odagi bandē

You accepted Kunti's prayers. As a friend of the Pandavas, You protected them day and night. Pleased with Prahlada's whole-hearted devotion, You delivered him from all trials and tribulations.

kanaka purandaradāsa gōrā-kumbārarigē
divya daruśana nīḍi dhanyara gaidē
nīn-olive ṣarat rahita bhakti prēmakē
karuṇisu ni namage jnāna mārgava

You blessed saints such as Kanakadasa, Purandaradasa and Gorakumbhar with Your darshan (divine vision). One may attain You through unconditional devotion. Please show us the way to divine wisdom.

indu habba (Baḍuga)

indu habba jana nanka ā mayakkaṇō
habba māṭuvō - āṭṭāṭuvō - ellā sinkarava irili

Today is a festival. Let us dance joyfully and celebrate. Let everyone be happy.

nankammā illi bandiyā
bandu nankava nōḍiyā
nōḍi nankava gavamāṭiyā
gavamāṭi nankava sinkaramāṭiya

Our Mother will come to see us all and shower Her love and make us happy.

ī lōka māyānta buḍisiya
ēkāntalē atu nanka hettē ammā...
habba māṭuvō - āṭṭāṭuvō - ellā sinkarava irili

She liberates us from delusion because She is our Mother. Let us dance and celebrate. May everyone be happy.

beṭṭa otaka rājiyamāṭūva hettē
binna bīsalu māṭibuḍu hettē
sīmēnō sinkarata enna dēvi – ninna
sinkara mukhava nōḍōduka āsabandarā

O Mother, who dwells on the mountain, please enlighten our lives. O most beautiful One in the Universe! We yearn to see Your beautiful face.

bhakti tā... bhakti tā... hettē
ninna śakti tandu badukuvē hettē
gavatā – gavatā – hettē
gavava tandu mayaksuvē hettē
nambikai tā... nambikai tā... hettē
nambikai tandu dāri tōrsuvē hettē

Mother, bless us with devotion and strength. Mother give us love, intoxicate us with Your love. Mother, give us faith and show us the right path.

indu habba jana nanka ā mayakkaṇō
habba māṭuvō – āṭṭāṭuvō – ellā sinkarava irili

Today is the festival day. Let us dance and celebrate. Let everyone be happy.

indukalā-dhara (Sanskrit)

indukalā-dhara gangā-jaṭā-dhara
śambhō śankara gaurīśa
sārasa-lōcana parimaḷa-gātra
pāvana-carita bhuvanēśvara

Shiva rules over time (lunar cycles to us) and wears the sacred river Ganga in His matted locks. Shambho, Shankara, Lord of Parvati! Shiva has lotus eyes, and is fragrant with the ash of renunciation. Your story is pure, O Lord of the world!

śambhō śankara śambhō śankara
śambhō śankara śivasambhō

O Shiva, source of eternal happiness.

dīna-dayāmaya dhīra parātpara
sāmba-sadāśiva mada-mathana
dēvadēva jaya sāmaja-varṇita
śūlapāṇē hṛdayēśvara

You are compassionate to the needy, the courageous One, the supreme. O Shiva, You churn our pride, and bring out our impurities. Victory to the God of gods, praised in the Sama Veda. You bear the trident 'trishula,' the perfect balance between male and female aspects, Lord of my heart.

parvata-nandinī priya-vadana sōma
sarva-layaṅkara jita-madana
karuṇālaya kailāsa-nivāsa
paripālaya mām paramēśvara

Beloved of Shakti, Your face radiates the intoxication of supreme knowledge. You annihilate all limitations and take all to the boundless state of consciousness. Abode of compassion, residing on Mount Kailasa, grant me refuge, Supreme Lord.

ini oru janmam (Tamil version)

ini oru piravi tārādē kṛṣṇā
madimōha cēril – kāl iḍari vīzhum

tarumenil nin bhakta aṭiyārkkaṭiyanāy
vāzhndiṭa enakkenḍrum varam vēṇḍumē

tirunāmam manadirkkuḷ niraivāga cey – kṛṣṇā
tirupāda malarenḍrum teḷivāga cey
sakalamum iraivā nin uruvāga tōnḍra cey
samanilai enḍrum en iyalpāga cey

kṛṣṇā... aruḷnidhiyē... tozhudēn unai... kai
tozhudēn... kai tozhudēn...

avanikku payanāgum vidhamāga cey – janmam
azhiyāda sukham nalgum vazhiyāga cey
anumadi adarkkāga tarumenil piravigaḷ
palanūr iniyum nī enakkaḷippāy

innentē vannilla (Malayalam)

innentē vannilla kaḷḷakkaṇṇan
mēcaka varṇṇanām uṇṇikkaṇṇan
ñānillā nērattu vannu-kērum
ñān vacca-veṇṇa kavarnnu pōkum
tiṇṇamuriyile maṇkalaṅgaḷ
onnillātellām uṭaccu-vakkyum
innentē vannilla kaḷḷakkaṇṇan
veṇṇa kavarunna kuññucōran
kuṭṭikkurumbā kaḷḷakkarumbā ōṭakkuzhal-ūti
cārē varu

Why hasn't the dark-hued Krishna, stealer of hearts, come today? He will come when I am not here, and steal the butter I made. He will smash all the clay pots in the courtyard. Why hasn't Krishna, stealer of hearts, come today? He is a little butter thief! O mischievous One, O darling thief, please come to me, playing your flute!

innīkkuṭilil nī vanniṭumbōḷ
vātil maraññu ñān nōkki-nilkkum
pīṭhamatilāyi ērininnā
veṇṇayum pālum kavarnniṭumbōḷ
cēlilāy ninne piṭiccu keṭṭum
kaṇṇu-kuḷirkkē ñān nōkki-nilkkum
innentē vannilla kaḷḷakkaṇṇan
amma yaśōda tan kaḷḷakkaṇṇan
kuṭṭikkurumbā kaḷḷakkarumbā ōṭakkuzhal-ūti
cārē varu

Today, I will hide behind the door to watch as You sneak into this hut. When You climb on the stool to steal the butter, I shall bind You with my robes and gaze at You to my heart's content. Stealer of hearts and Mother Yashoda's darling, why haven't You come today? O mischievous One, O darling thief, please come to me, playing Your flute!

sūryan paṭiññāru cenn-aṇaññu
kālikaḷ mēññu tiriccu vannu
ñān vecca veṇṇa niram pakarnnu
kaṇṇil-eriyum tiriyum keṭṭu
ñānillā nērattu mātram-āṇō
nī vannu pōkuka ende kaṇṇā
amma yaśōdakkyu mātramallī
ninne puṇaruvānuḷḷa bhāgyam

kuṭṭikkurumbā kaḷḷakkarumbā ōṭakkuzhal-ūti
cārē varu

The sun has set in the west, and the cows have returned from grazing. The color of the butter I prepared has changed. The light in my eyes has gone out. O my dear Krishna, will You come and go only when I am absent? Is the good fortune of hugging You reserved only for Mother Yashoda? O mischievous One, O darling thief, please come to me, playing Your flute!

iṇṭilōkki (Telugu)

iṇṭi lōkki vacināḍē – cinnāri kṛṣṇā - manassu lōki vacināḍē
iṇṭilōkki vacināḍu manassuloki vacināḍu
vennalanni dōcināḍē –
cinnāri kṛṣṇā manasulanni dōcināḍē

Little Krishna entered my house and heart. He entered the house and stole the butter. He entered my heart and stole my heart. Little Krishna stole our hearts!

uṭṭipaina vennamuntta gollabhāmā
cekkucedara-kuṇḍinādē
uṭṭipaina munttalū cekkucedar- kuṇḍenū
vennamudda kānarādē – cinnāri kṛṣṇā
vennalanni dōcināḍē

O milkmaid, the pots hanging from the roof seem undisturbed, yet the butter is missing. Surely little Krishna has entered the house and stolen all the butter!

impaina mōmuvāḍē cinnikṛṣṇā
sompugā navvēvāḍē

impaina mōmutō sompugā navvutū
manassulō dūrināḍē – cinnāri kṛṣṇā
manassunē dōcināḍē

With His beautiful face and enchanting smile, he entered my heart. Little Krishna stole my heart.

iruḷil ninnuṭal (Malayalam)

iruḷil ninnuṭal cumaṭum cummi
varunn-iviṭēkkyu manuṣyan
niravadhi karma-gatikk-anurūpam
iruḷil pōyaṭiyunnu

Owing to the darkness of ignorance, man comes to this world bearing the burden of his body. After a life of experiencing the fruits of his actions, he returns to darkness again.

arutivaruttān ariyārutātī
gamanāgamanam tuṭarum
jīvitam-ennum-anātham palakuri
jani-mṛti-cakram-uruṇḍu

Until man gains the right knowledge, he will continue to come and go. The wheel of life and death rolls on relentlessly, and life continues without any support.

taṅgaḷil-ariyunn-illatum-alla
avan-ariyunnill-avane
sahayātrikar-ennālum paricitar-
allakamizhiyil timiram

Man does not know himself, his true essence. The vision of his companions, who are also ignorant of the Self, remains clouded by the cataracts of ignorance.

paramānanda pālkkaṭal-uḷḷil
alañoriyunnuṇḍarivāy
ariyān sadayam kṛpayaruḷiṭān
gurucaraṇam tān śaraṇam

The milky waves of the ocean of supreme bliss are within your own Self. To realize my true Self, I seek refuge, that She may bestow Her grace upon me. I seek refuge at my Guru's feet.

iruḷ māri teḷiyānāyi (Malayalam)

iruḷ māri teḷiyānāyi itaḷ-uḷḷam viriyānāyi
iniyentinn-aruḷīṭān, kaniyēṇamē, ammē
tuṇayēkaṇē

O Mother, shower Your grace and tell me how to transform my darkness into light and make my heart blossom. Please be with me!

vazhiyēre alaññu-pōy, kara-kāṇātulaññu pōyi
mizhi-tūki kara-kērān, iṭayākaṇē ammē
tuṇayēkaṇē

In anguish I wandered along many paths, never seeing the shore. O Mother, guide me to the shore. Please be with me!

mati-mōham vaḷarunnu, gati-vēgam kurayunnu
guṇam-ēkān nara-janmam, gatiyēkaṇē ammē
tuṇayēkaṇē

Desires are growing and the journey is slowing. O Mother, guide me to fulfill my human birth. Please be with me!

hṛdi-vīṇayil śruticērān, para-bhaktiyil layam-ēkān
nirayēṇam mama manasē, padamēkaṇē ammē
tuṇayēkaṇē

Fill my heart O Mother, to tune the veena of my heart and to merge in the melody of supreme devotion. Please be with me!

jagadambā prēmānē (Marathi)

jagadambā prēmānē, āhē bōlāvat
āyī āpulī āhē vāṭ pahāt
antarīcyā andharācā, karuṇiyā ant
prēmadīp sarvāntarī, karunī pradīpt
jagadambā... jagadambā...

With open arms Mother calls everyone. The divine Mother comes to Her children to end their misery and to light the lamp of pure love.

madhur hāsya mātṛmukhī vilasat
prēm vātsalya nayanī zaḷakat
dēyunī karm, bhaktī jñānāmṛt
śikavitē sugam sādhanārīt
jagadambā... jagadambā...

Her unparalleled smile lights up her face. Her eyes shine with love and compassion for Her children. By teaching devotees about karma, bhakti and jnana (paths of action, devotion and knowledge), She encourages them to go beyond body and mind.

mīpaṇ visarūnī, visāvū kavēt
visambūnī āyīvar hōvūyā niścint
nirmaḷ prēmācā anubhav ghēt

jāṇā jagadambā, nitya śōbhat
jagadambā... jagadambā...

Forgetting ourselves, let us rest in Her arms. Surrendering everything, let us be free from all worries. While experiencing pure love, let us understand that God is our own (we belong to God).

nisvārtth sēvēcī kās dharat
bhakti-bhāvānē nitya māttēlā bhajat
sadā sarvāñcī, sukhaśānti cintat
dhāran karū jagadambā hṛdayāt
jagadambā... jagadambā...

Let us take the path of selfless service and sing the Divine Mother's name with devotion. While praying for peace and happiness for all beings, let us hold Mother in our hearts.

jagatanātha (Odiya)

jagatanātha prabhū jagannātha hē
jagatanātha prabhū jagannātha

You are the saviour of the universe, O Lord Jagannath!

patita pābana hari e bhabaru debe tāri
apalaka caka ākhi ḍākuthānti bāhu ṭeki
otharē alapa hasa dayā jara jara mukha
sabū saṅkaṭū phiṭāibē bāṭa he

The saviour of the downtrodden will save us from samsara. With wide open eyes and raised arms he calls us. Behold his soft smile and compassionate face. He will show us the way out of all problems.

deuḷe na lāge mana chāḍi ratna siṁhāsana
rucenā chapana bhōga dhūpa dīpa bhōga rāga
bhakatara snehā ghāre ḍāka subhē bāre bāre
āsa sāī karibā misi jāta he

He is not happy inside the temple or sitting on the bejewelled throne. Nor does he enjoy the prasad offerings or puja rituals. He is moved by the love of his devotees who call out, "Come, O Lord, let's celebrate together." (Rath Yatra)

bada deulū bāhāri bhakata bhiḍā re gherī
dese dese nagarare bulibe āji ṭhākure
nija racilā saṁsāre ṭaṇā hebe māyā ḍore
saja bāja helāṇi tini ratha he

He comes out of the temple surrounded by devotees. Today He will roam the world, pulled by the bonds of maya through the samsara that He Himself created. Look, the chariots (for the Rath Yatra) are all decorated and ready.

jaya jaya śankara (Kannada)

jaya jaya śankara jaya abhayaṅkara
gaja carmāmbara jaya gaṅgādhara
pāhi pāhi paramēśā
pāhi pāhi viśvēśā

Victory to the auspicious One, who dispels fear, who is garbed in an elephant hide, who bears the Ganges on His head! Protect me, O supreme Lord, Lord of the Universe!

triśūla-dhāriyē ḍamaruga pāṇiyē
śaśidharanē paraśiva haranē

dayāmūrttiyē...
ōm śiva ōm śiva ōm śiva ōm
dayāmūrttiyē agaṇita mahimanē
vāmadēva jaya rudrēśā

O Supreme One, you wield the trident in one hand, and the damaru (drum) in the other. The crescent moon adorns your matted locks. O embodiment of compassion, You are ever auspicious. O compassionate One, your glory is incomparable. Victory to Vamadeva (sustainer of the universe) of terrifying form!

pāhi pāhi paramēśā
pāhi pāhi viśvēśā

Protect me, O supreme Lord, Lord of the Universe!

sumanasa vandita sundarēśanē
bēḍuvēv-anudina amarēśā
moreyanālisi...
ōm śiva ōm śiva ōm śiva ōm
moreyanālisi salahū nammanu
bhava-bhayahara hē bhīmēśā

Most handsome One, You are worshipped by the pious. Immortal One, I pray to You daily. O Shiva, please hear my heartfelt call and protect me. O mighty One, You destroy the fear of samsara (cycle of birth and death).

jīvitam-ennoru tuṭarkatha (Malayalam)

jīvitam-ennoru tuṭarkatha
pariṇāmattin perumkatha

tuṭakkam-eviṭe? oṭukkam-eviṭe?
piṭuttamillā-kaṭam-katha

Life is an ongoing story, a great tale of evolution. Where is its beginning, where is its end? This is a mystery to which no one has the answer.

aṭutt-ariññavar-urakkey-ōti
atinde tanirūpam
'avācyam-ākum suśāntam-ākum'
atinde nijabhāvam

The Self-realized who know it well proclaim its true nature out loud. "It is pure, infinite, peace and bliss."

bōdham... atu bōdham..

Awareness, it is awareness.

avar mozhiññu: 'manass-aṭakki
ariññu-koḷḷuka niṅgaḷ'
manass-aṭakkām-ananta-saukhyam
nukarnn-amartyata pūkām

They said, "Still your mind and know it well." Let us still our mind, enjoy infinite bliss and become immortal.

jīvita ommē (Kannada)

jīvita ommē hindē mundē
tirugi ommē nōḍidarē
dhanyavāda ammā ninagē
dhanyavāda ammā...

If we look back at our lives and see how we fared, all we can do is say a heartfelt "Thank you" to You, O Mother.

ninna neraḷigē ninna pālanegē
ninna kāruṇyakkē vātsalyakkē
hēḷalu uṇṭu nanagē – dēvī
hāḍalu uṇṭu nanagē
dhanyavāda ammā ninagē
dhanyavāda ammā...

O Devi, for the love and care You have provided, for the grace You have showered upon us—for all that, Mother, I can only say, "Thank you."

ninna kṛpegē ninna vīkṣaṇege
ninna śikṣaṇake rakṣaṇege
hēḷalu uṇṭu nanagē – dēvī
hāḍalu uṇṭu nanagē
dhanyavāda ammā ninagē
dhanyavāda ammā

O Devi, for the lessons You have taught us, for the shelter You have given, and the way You protect us — all I can do is say, "Thank you."

jñāna-dīpam (Malayalam)

jñāna-dīpam teḷikkū, manassē nī
bhēda-bhāvam tyajikkū
sānandam-ambikaye, nirantaram
antarangē bhajikkyū

O mind, light the lamp of wisdom and let go of duality. Always worship the divine Mother blissfully.

mānābhimānam-ellām duḥkha-pradam
nānātva-buddhi-mūlam
santatam cinta-ceyyū, itallayō
cinta-pōkkunna cinta

From duality comes pride and ego which then cause sorrow. Constantly contemplate on this and it will remove all other thoughts.

dēham veṭiññu dēhi pōkunnēram
mōham kalarnniṭāte
bhaktyā japicciṭēṇam, bhayāpaham
durgadurgēti mantram

When the soul leaves the body, freed from delusion, you should chant 'Durga, Durga' with devotion. This will remove all fears.

kīzh-mēl maraññu-lōkam, satyam-innu-
nāma-mātram vicitram
lōkāśa vēṇḍa cittē, śōkam vinā
lōkēśiye ninakkyū

The world has turned upside-down and truth has become a mere word. O mind, leave worldly pleasures and, free of sorrow, remember the Mother of the world.

kāminī-kāñcanaṅgaḷ manam kāṭṭum
māya-tan sambhramaṅgaḷ
svāntamē santyajikkū, amaratva
dhanyataye varikkū

Lust and wealth are mere projections of the mind. O mind, leave them and reach deathlessness.

jōt jalālē rām (Hindi)

śrī rām rām rāmēti ramē rāmē manōramē
sahasra-nāma tat tulyam rāma-nāma varānanē

By chanting the name of Rama, my mind gets lost in the divine consciousness of the Lord.

jōt jalālē rām kī man mēṅ
sab viṣayōṅ kē andhiyārē taj
rām rām bas rām rām bhaj
rām rām bas rām rām bhaj

Light the sacred flame of Rama within. Give up the darkness of worldly objects. Just chant the name Rama Rama.

sab rōgōṅ kī auṣadh rāmā
har uljhan kī suljhan rāmā
rām rām... bōlō rām rām...
rām rām... bōlō rām rām...
jab bhī saṅkaṭ sē ghir jāyē
man paglē tū rām rām bhaj
rām rām bas rām rām bhaj
rām rām bas rām rām bhaj

He is the cure for all ailments. Chanting "Rama Rama" solves all problems. Whenever you are immersed in sorrow, O foolish mind, just chant Rama's name, just chant the name "Rama Rama."

madhur nahi kōyi gīt rām sā
nikaṭ nahīṅ kōyi mīt rāmsā
rām rām... bōlō rām rām...
rām rām... bōlō rām rām...

amrit madhumay jīvan cāhē
rām rām ras rōm rōm rac
rām rām bas rām rām bhaj
rām rām bas rām rām bhaj

No song is sweeter than Rama. No friend is closer than Rama. Just chant "Rama Rama." To experience immortality in your life, just revel in the sweet name of Rama until every atom within you resounds with Him. Just chant "Rama Rama"...

rām nām bin jñān na kōyi
rām chōḍ vijñān na kōyi
rām rām... bōlō rām rām...
rām rām... bōlō rām rām...
jagati kē sab bhēd khulēṅgē
rām nām kā karlē jap tap
rām rām bas rām rām bhaj
rām rām bas rām rām bhaj

Without the name of Rama there is no knowledge. Without Rama there is no wisdom. Chant "Rama Rama." All the secrets of the world will be revealed. Just chant and meditate on the name Rama. Just chant "Ram Ram."

rām ki mahimā yōgi gāvē
bhagat rām bhaj rām hi pāvē
rām rām... bōlō rām rām...
rām rām... bōlō rām rām...
prabh kā pāvan mandir ban jā
niś din pal pal rām nām bhajō
rām rām bas rām rām bhaj

rām rām bas rām rām bhaj

The yogis sing the glories of Rama. The devotee who chants Rama gains the Lord. Chant "Ram Ram." Be a pure temple of the Lord. Each day, each moment chant the name Rama. Just chant "Ram Ram."

rām rām bōlō rām rām
rām rām bas rām rām bhaj
rām rām bas jay jay rām
rām rām bōlō rām rām

kaisā nāc nacāyā (Hindi)

kaisā nāc nacāyā... ri māyā
kaisā nāc nacāyā
khōj mēṅ sukh ki is jag mēṅ
aisē bhramaṇ karāyā... ri māyā...

O Maya, how you made us dance to your tune. In search of happiness in this world, you made us wander all over.

hāḍ mās kē is piñjarē kō
kēval satya batāyā
maiṅ mērā kē bhāv kō tūnē
nit balavān banāyā... ri māyā

You led us to believe that this cage of bone and flesh is the only reality. O Maya, you kept strengthening our sense of 'I' and 'mine'.

jab āyē duḥkh jīvan mēṅ tō
mārg galat dikhlāyā
viṣayōṅ mēṅ geharē ḍūb rē manvā
aisā pāṭh paḍhāyā - ri māyā

When sufferings came, you showed us the wrong paths. You taught us to immerse ourselves yet deeper in worldly pleasures.

khēl tabhī yē khatam huā jab
sadguru caraṇ kō pāyā
unkī apār kṛpā sē antar
sukh aisā mainē pāyā
nit man ānand mē harṣāyā

When I reached the feet of the Sadguru, this game of yours was over. By the Guru's grace I found inner bliss and my mind is submerged in eternal happiness!

kāj karō (Hindi)

kāj karō nit jan sēvā kē
sēvā mēṅ prabhu kē darśan haiṅ
kāj karō... kāj karō...

Always engage yourself in the service of others, as service leads to the vision of the Lord.

sēvā dil mēṅ pyār jagātī
sēvā hi bhakti janmāti
sēvā mēṅ hī gyān kā phal hai
sēvā sē miltē bhagavan haiṅ

Service awakens love in our hearts and paves the way for devotion. Service brings the fruits of wisdom. Service brings us the Lord Himself!

sēvā se caltā jag sārā
sēvā hī prakṛti kā nārā
anathak sēvā mēṅ rat sārē

cānd sūraj sab tārāgaṇ haiṅ

The whole world runs on the basis of service. It is the way of Nature itself. The moon, sun and stars all tirelessly serve!

svārth karm sē man bandh jāyē
anagin janmōṅ mēṅ bhaṭkāyē
sēvā kāraj kā mārag hī
citta kī śuddhi kā sādhan haiṅ

Selfish actions bind the mind and cause transmigration. Serving is the way to purify our mind.

Kāḷī dēvī, mother to me (English)

Kāḷī dēvī, mother to me,
Jaganmātā Bhairavī,
Show me your form.

Within your eyes the world is created.
Out of your mouth flows the song of the Truth.
Forgotten in time, revived by the sages
down through the ages, to guide our way home...
to guide our way home...

Through endless lives your voice of eternity
floods in my memory, opens my mind.
Within every form, you're dancing in front of me,
silently showing the purpose of life...
the purpose of life...

Since timeless past we seek to find you

in distant shrines and mountain caves.
Beyond the reach of what is fated
this dream of life, your wondrous play...
your wondrous play...

kāḷi kāḷi kāḷi kālasvarūpiṇi (Telugu)

kāḷi kāḷi kāḷi kālasvarūpiṇi kāḷi
kāḷi kāḷi kāḷi trilōka-janani kāḷi

O Kali, You are of the nature of Time. You are the mother of the three worlds.

trikālamulanu sṛṣṭiñcina kāḷi
kāla cakramunu naḍuputunna kāḷi
nīla kaṇṭuni ēdapai nilacina kāḷi
kālamu cellina kapālamulu dhariñcu kāḷi

O Kali, You created the past, present and future. You drive the wheel of time. O Kali, You stand on the chest of the blue-necked Shiva. You are adorned by skulls which represent time.

jagamunu mingutunna śyāmavarṇa kāḷi
śivaśaktulu ēkamai nilacivunna kāḷi
jñāna-khaḍgamu cēpaṭṭina kāḷi
triśūlamutō triguṇamāyanu cēdiñcu kāḷi

O dark-skinned Kali, You swallow the world. You are a manifestation of Shiva-Shakti (the union of masculine and feminine energies). You wield the sword of knowledge. With your trident, You sever the three gunas (sattva, rajas and tamas).

manuṣya ahamunu tanapiḍikililō dhariñcina kāḷi
bhakti-vivēka vairāgyamulu prasādiñce kāḷi
amma ani ārtitōpilicina karuṇiñce kāḷi
tanabiḍḍalanu amṛtapadamuna nilipē kāḷi

O Kali, You hold the human ego in your hand. You bestow devotion, discernment and dispassion. You bestow your grace on the one who devoutly calls out, "Mother!" You shower your children with immortal bliss.

jay jay kāḷi mahākāḷi jay jay kāḷi
jay jay kāḷi kapāli kāḷi jay jay kāḷi
jay jay kāḷi bhairavi kāḷi jay jay kāḷi
jay jay kāḷi cāmuṇḍi kāḷi jay jay kāḷi

Victory to the great Kali, victory to Kali adorned with the garland of skulls. Victory to Kali, who is awe-inspiring. Victory to the fearsome Kali!

kamanīya-rūpan (Malayalam)

kamanīya-rūpanen kārmēgha-varṇṇan
karuṇāmayan-eṅgu pōyi?
karayum manassine praṇayikkum maṇivarṇṇan
karayuvān viṭṭeṅgu pōyi?

O beautiful Lord, the compassionate one of the color of rain clouds, where have You gone? Lord Krishna loves the heart that cries in love for Him. Where has He gone, leaving us to cry?

ī vazhikkeṅgānen jīva-caitanyamām
kārvarṇṇan-eṅgānum kaṭannu-pōyō?
viṇṇitil ōḍi kaḷiccu rasikkumā-
nīla-mēghattōṭu ārāññavaḷ

nīla-mēghattōṭu ārāññavaḷ

Has the Lord, radiant as the rain cloud, the life within me, passed this way? She asked of the blue clouds floating merrily in the sky, "Did He pass by this way?"

eviṭeyō ponkāl cilambocca kēṭṭapōl
pāzhiruṭṭattu naṭannu rādha
eviṭeyō kaḷavēṇu nisvanam kēṭṭatu –
rāvinde māril tiraññu rādha
rāvinde māril tiraññu rādha

When Radha heard the tinkling of anklets, she walked out in the darkness. She heard the melodious sound of the flute and searched for her Lord in the heart of the night.

mādhava-mānasa mōhananē śrīdhara kēśava yādavanē
pāvana nīla-kaḷēbaranē gōkula-nāyaka pāhi harē

O Madhava (consort of Mahalakshmi), You are the beauty within my heart. O Sridhara (most auspicious one), O Keshava (slayer of the demon Keshi), O Yadavane (of the lineage of Yadus)! O divine One with radiant blue body, the Lord of Gokula, I take refuge in You.

murivēttu nīrunna pēlava mānasam
kaṇṇande nāmattil ūnni ninnu
tannātma-nāthane cinticcu cinticcu
kaṇṇunīr-āzhiyil muṅgi ninnu
kaṇṇunīr-āzhiyil muṅgi ninnu

The tender heart, wounded by love for Krishna, held fast to the Lord by constantly remembering his name. Thinking intensely of the Lord of her soul, she shed profuse tears.

tāraṅgaḷ mānattu tīrttorā pūttālam
tāmara-poykayil nōkki nilkke
mānasa-poykayil tāmara-kaṇṇande
malaraṭi-rādha teḷiññu-kaṇḍu
malaraṭi-rādha teḷiññu-kaṇḍu

She stood looking at the reflection of the stars in the lake of lotus flowers. The holy feet of her lotus-eyed Lord dawned clearly in the lake of Radha's heart.

kaṇā kaṇā (Marathi)

kaṇā kaṇā madhē kṛṣṇ kanhaiyyā rōm rōmāt rām rē
kṣaṇōkṣaṇi jīvan dēyi tō nij sarvānca saṅgi rē

You (Sri Krishna, Sri Rama) are the constant companion in and throughout everything in the Universe.

śruti sāṅgatē saccidānand tō sarvāntaryāmi rē
svayamprakāś tū sarvātmā rē nij paramātmā tūca rē
sarv-vyāpt tū...
sarv-vyāpt tū dēhaśrōtrādi pañcēndriyādi pār rē
avyakt hi tū nirākār rē tūhi kṛṣṇ rām rē
bōlā rām rām rām sītā rām rām rām
bōlā śyām śyām śyām rādhē śyām śyām śyām

Scriptures reveal You are Brahman (existence-consciousness-bliss) and the indwelling soul of all. You are also the self-illumining Self of all, the all-pervading Supreme Self, beyond all experiences, unmanifest and devoid of all forms. You are the very Krishna Rama.

tujhē svarūp asē divya he vṛthā vyathita bhrānt rē
nāhi agamya ēkhi sādhan kēvaḷ guru upadēś rē
nityaśuddh tū...
nityaśuddh tū buddh mukt hi sarv-sākṣi
paramārtha rē
jīvansār hēca satya rē tūhi kṛṣṇ rām rē
bōlā rām rām rām sītā rām rām rām
bōlā śyām śyām śyām rādhē śyām śyām śyām

You are deluded and disquieted despite your exalted true nature. The way to realize this is not incomprehensible. Guru Upadesh is the only way. You are eternal, ever pure, all knowing, the ever-liberated witness of all, the supreme Truth. This is the very essence of life, Krishna re Rama re.

kaṇṇā nin vēṇu (Malayalam)

kaṇṇā nin vēṇu-gānāmṛta-lahariyil
rādhayāyīṭunnu en hṛdantam
nī vannu pāṭi uṇartti-en mānasam
vṛndāvanikayāy pūv-aṇiññu

O Krishna, my heart has become Radha, intoxicated by the melody of Your flute. You awakened my heart with your song and it has blossomed like the gardens of Vrindavan.

oru nūru puṣpa-vṛndaṅgaḷ viṭarunnu
oru nūru paiṅkiḷi pāṭiṭunnu
oru prēma-yamuna-en uḷḷil-ozhukunnu
gōpikamār nṛttam-āṭiṭunnu kaṇṇā...
kaṇṇā...

Flowers bloom in hundreds, and a hundred little birds sing. The Yamuna has become a river of love within me and the gopis dance, O Krishna.

paikkaḷ karayunnu ānanda-lahariyil
gōkulam-ākunnu bhū-maṇḍalam
pāṭi aṇayunnu manda-samīranum
pāṭunnu nin prēma-vēṇu-gānam
kaṇṇā...

The cows call out in blissful intoxication. The entire earth has become Gokulam (where Krishna spent his childhood). The gentle breeze also rejoices, singing the flute-song of your love.

sarva carācaram ninnil-āmagnarāy
ēkātma saṅgīta-dhārayāy
nityamām ānanda-svara-rāga-dhārayil
ñān tanne enne marannitaṭṭe
kaṇṇā...

All beings, sentient and non-sentient, are absorbed in You, and they unite into One in the flow of Your music. May I ever forget myself in the blissful melody that flows from Your flute!

kaṇṇan-en cārattu (Malayalam)

kaṇṇan-en cāratt-aṇaññiṭumbōḷ
ñān-oru rādhayāy cērnnu nilkkum
kaṇṇan muraḷika-ūtiṭumbōḷ
gōpikayāyi ñān nṛttam-āṭum

When Kannan comes near me, I will stand close to him, as a Radha. When he plays his flute, I will dance as a gopi.

kaṇṇā kaṇṇā gōpakumārā
muraḷilōlā rāgavilōlā

O Kannan, young cowherd, player of the flute, loving one!

kāḷindi tīrattu kaṇṇanumāy
gōkkaḷe mēccu rasicciṭum ñān
kaṇṇan maraññu kaḷaññiṭumbōḷ
kaṇṇunīr tūki ñān kāttirikkum

Along with Kannan, I will delight in taking the cows to graze on the banks of the Kalindi river. When Kannan disappears, I will wait and shed tears.

kaṇṇande-āgamam vaikiyennāl
uṇṇāt-uraṅgāt-uzhanniṭum ñān
kaṇṇan-ennuḷḷil viḷaṅgi-ennāl
kaṇṇanum ñānum abhinnarallō

If Kannan delays in coming, in distress I will forgo food and sleep. When Kanna shines within me, then Kannan and I become one being.

kaṇṇirkkaṭalin karayil (Malayalam)

kaṇṇir-kkaṭalin karayil viriññoru
puñciripp̄uvu nī ammē
kāṇān koticc-alayunnū – naṣṭa
nāvikanāyi ñān ninne

O Mother, you are a smiling flower blooming on the shore of the ocean of my tears. I am like a wandering, lost boatman, thirsting to see You.

ninn-ōrmma-ēkiṭum harṣam – onnē
ī janma vēnalil varṣam
en kayyil ninnum niyati – atu
taṭṭi-eṭukkān viṭallē

The delight of remembering You is a rain shower in the scorching summer of my life. Please do not let fate steal this from me.

nirmala bhaktikku mātram – kēzhum
ennuḍe sādhu cittattil
nīḷum nirāśā nizhal nīkkaṇē – nin
kṛpākānti cintum kaṭākṣam

My desolate mind cries out for pure devotion alone. Please remove the dark shadows of hopelessness by Your radiant grace-filled glance.

kūriruḷ peyyunnu vānam – cuttum
cīrum koṭuṅkātt-apāram
dūreyāy kāṇmū ñān dēvī – nin
kōṭīratāram pozhikkum prakāśam

The sky rains darkness, and hurricanes blow all around me. O Devi, the brilliant effulgence of the stars in Your crown guide me from afar.

karaḷ niraññu (Malayalam)

karaḷ niraññu mizhi niraññu
mozhi marannu ninnu ñān
pūnilāvin prabha coriññu
munnil nī vann-aṇayavē

With full heart and brimming eyes, I stood wonder-struck as You came before me, with the radiance of the full moon.

kaṇḍu nin tū-mandahāsam
iruḷ-akannu pulariyāy
pāḍi pūṅkuyil praṇaya
madhura sāndra gītakam
hima-kaṇaṅgaḷ peytiraṅgi
hṛdaya-sarayū tīravum
nanavariññu mṛdulamāy
viṭarnnu pūvitaḷukaḷ

Seeing your beautiful, soft smile, darkness gives way to light. O eternal one, the song-bird sings of the sweetness of Your love. Dew drops soak the shores of the river of my heart, and flowers bloom softly in your wake.

sirakaḷ nirayum prēma-bhakti
lahariyāy paṭarnniṭum
dhārayūrnnu dhanyamāy
nityam-uḷḷil nirayū nī
amṛtamāyī puṇya-janmam
ninnil-onnu cēruvān
ātmabōdha niravilūṭe
svayam-ariññu uṇarnniṭān

Ambrosial waves of love and devotion fill my entire being, and my life is forever blessed. May my life merge into You and become immortal. May I awaken in my Self, and be established in the knowledge of the Self.

ammē... ammē... ammē... ammē...

kar-lē dhyān tu bandē (Hindi)

kar-lē dhyān tu bandē

kar-lē dhyān tu bandē

O man! meditate ...

kyōṅ bhaṭakē tū, bāhar bāhar
jō tu ḍhūṇḍē vō hai andar
viṣayōṅ kē pīchē, kyōṅ tu bhāgē
jag mē tēra kuch na lāgē

Why are you searching for things outside? What you seek is within you. Why do you run after the vishayas (sense objects)? Nothing in this world belongs to you.

manō-buddhi-ahaṅkār dēha tū nahīṅ
svapna tū nahīṅ, jāgrat tū nahīṅ
tū hai ātma, jān lē ab tō
saccidānanda hai, mān lē ab tō

You are not the mind, body, ego or senses. Neither are you the dream state nor the waking state. You are Atma. Know this now and realize that you are Satchidananda.

yē sansār haiṅ, adbhut māyā
sac bhi jhūṭh bhī, jaisē chāyā
jō sadguru ki, śaraṇ mēṅ āyē
māyā uskō, pakaḍ na pāyē

This world is an amazing maya (illusion), both false as well as true, just like the shadow. But this maya cannot catch one who takes refuge in the Guru.

sōham... śivōham
sōham... śivōham
tattvamasi... śivam advaitam

I am that ... I am Shiva. Thou art that ... One with Shiva.

kārmukil varṇṇande līlakaḷ (Malayalam)

kārmukil varṇṇande līlakaḷ-ōrōnnum
cintayil varṇam vitariṭunnu
cārutayārnnorā mandasmitam ende
antaraṅgattinnu harṣōtsavam

The divine plays of my Lord, who is the color of a dark rain-cloud, paint my thoughts in lovely colors. My mind leaps up in joyful celebration as I remember the radiant beauty of his smile.

kuyilinde kūjanam kēḷkkumbōḷ-ōrkkum ñān
gōpakumārande vēṇu-nādam
kārmukil mānam nirayumbōḷ – kāroḷi
varṇande sānnidhyamāya pōle

The songs of the koel remind me of the melodies flowing from the young cowherd's flute. When dark rain-clouds cover the sky, I feel the presence of my dark-hued Lord.

maṇṇu-vāri-ttinna kaṇṇane-ōrttu pōm
muttattu piñcu-paitaṅgaḷ ninnāl
paikkaḷā muttatu-mēññu naṭakkumbōḷ
ōrttiṭum gōpāla-bālanē ñān

When I see little children in the front yard, I remember the young Krishna who ate mud. I remember my young cowherd when cows graze in my front yard.

kuññuṅgaḷ kūṭi kaḷikkumbōḷ-ōrttiṭum

vṛndāvanattile līlakaḷ ñān
prēma-gānaṅgaḷ-en karṇṇattil-ettumbōḷ
rādha-tan prēmatte-ōrttu pōkum

I remember the divine sports of Vrindavan when small children play together. When I hear love songs, I remember Radha's supreme love for Krishna.

nāmam japiccitām nanmakaḷ ceytiṭām
kaṇṇande gōpanmārāyi mārām
vṛndāvanattile līlakaḷ-ōrttōrttu
kṛṣṇanil līnarāyi tīrnnu pōkām

We will chant his name, we will do good, and we will become Kanna's gopas (cowherds). Remembering the leelas in Vrindavan, we will finally merge in Krishna.

kārtikēya subrahmaṇya (Telugu)

kārtikēya subrahmaṇya murugaiyyā
skanda-tēja śaravaṇa-bhava daṇḍa-pāṇī

O Lord Kartikeya, Subrahmanya, Muruga! (names of Muruga.) O Saravanabhava. Your radiant form holds a spear.

kuṇḍalinī kadaliñcu vallināthā
indriyamulanu sāsiñcu dēva-sēnāpatē
nēnevarō... nēnevarō...
nēnevarō nēnevarō bōdhiñcu guruguha
ārudiśala caitanya-mūrtti ṣaṇmukha

Lord of Valli, You awaken the yogic kundalini power within us. Lord of the deva army, you control the sense organs. You are Guruguha, dwelling deep within us and teaching us the knowledge 'who am I?'. O Lord of six faces, You are the embodiment of all-pervading consciousness.

śaravaṇabhava śaravaṇabhava śaraṇabhava ōm
śaravaṇabhava śaravaṇabhava śaraṇabhava ōm

O Lord Saravanabhava!

śivaśaktyaikya-rūpa kumāra-svāmi
vākpaṭhimaniccu gaṇēśa-sōdara
mōhana-sundarā... mōhana-sundarā...
mayūra-vāhanācarā mōhanasundarā
tārakāsura samhāra śūladhāri

You are in the form of a child, and You are in the form of the union of Shiva and Shakti. You are the brother of Ganesh manifesting within us as the power of speech. Your beautiful, enchanting form travels on a peacock and You carry the spear that killed the demon Tarakasura.

karuṇayinda (Kannada)

karuṇayinda ā kaṇgaḷu nōḍitu
tumbi tuḷukitu dayāsāgara
ālaṅgisidaḷu prati kaṇa kaṇa
tanna bāhugaḷalli ettikkoṇḍu
ā divya sparśavu nīḍitu niratiśaya ānanda

Those eyes looked (at me) with compassion. The ocean of compassion overflowed; She took me in Her arms, embracing every cell. That divine touch gave me incomparable bliss.

cētanagoṇḍitu jīva ā kṣaṇavu

dik bhramevāyitu manasu
hṛdaya araḷitu ā kṣaṇavu
prapañcada ākarṣaṇe hōyitu

Then my soul was rejuvenated, my mind was stunned, my heart blossomed and all worldly attractions fell away.

jaya jaya paramēśvari paramārttha
jaya jaya paramēśvari paramārttha

ā prēmadalli ellā ondāyitu
ammā... ammā... ammā...
ā prēmadalli ellā ondāyitu ā kṣaṇavu
ellā śabdagaḷu niśśabdavāyitu
ellā śabdagaḷu niśśabdavāyitu
svarga sukhagaḷu tuccha eṇisitu
ellavu śūnya eṇisitu ā kṣaṇavu

In that love everything became one. All sounds ceased. Heavenly pleasures became despicable, and everything became void.

ātmakke amṛta sikkidantāyitu
ammā... ammā... ammā...
ellā tīrtthakṣētra puṇya sikkitu
jīvitadalli divyatvavu mūḍitu
jñāna hṛdayadalli udayavāyitu

Then my soul filled with nectar, and I received the merit of visiting all sacred places. Sacredness entered life in that moment, and wisdom dawned in the heart.

kṛṣṇaghanā rē (Marathi)

kṛṣṇaghanā rē kṛṣṇaghanā
bhijavaśīla kā rē mājhyā manā
kṛṣṇaghanā rē kṛṣṇaghanā...

O dark cloud, won't you drench my mind?

śubhra śubhra ḍhagāñcyā āḍūna
ēk kṛṣṇa ghana disatō madhūna
hasatō divya tyā śalākātūna
jagadambāca disatē maza tyātūna

In the midst of many white clouds, one dark one laughs through the divine lightning and I see the Divine Mother smiling through it.

āī bhavānī jaya jagadambē
dēvi śivānī śāradā vandē

Victory to Mother Bhavani, the Mother of the Universe! Prostrations to Goddess Shivani (consort of Lord Shiva) and Sharada (Goddess of Learning)!

kitī disāncā mī tahānalēlā
ēkāki jīva kāsāvīsa zhālā
tvarā yēūna tava jaladhārātūna
karaśīla kā āī amṛt siñcana

This lonely one has been thirsty and restless for so many days. Won't You come quickly, O Mother, and shower on me the nectar of immortality?

udāsa ritē hē māzhē mana
dēṇāra mī kōṇa kōṭhūna

akṣaya tujhyā prēm pātrātūna
dēśīla kā āī tū bharūna

My mind is sad and empty. What can I possibly give anyone? O Mother, won't You fill my mind from your ever-full jar of love?

kuṭilam-ākum (Malayalam)

kuṭilam-ākum-adharmam perukavē
koṭiya-pātakam-eṅgum vaḷaravē
janani! nī vannu dharmam pularttuvān
avani dhanyayāy ammē! jaganmayī!
avani dhanyayāy ammē! jaganmayī!

Unrighteousness flourishes and sinful deeds increase. O Mother, You have come to restore dharma, and the world is blessed.

uriyāṭiyilla onnu nī pāvanī
dharayil janmam-eṭuttoru vēḷayil
'karayānuḷḷat-allī martya-jīvitam'
itu nī maunamāy mantriccat-āvumō?

O holy One, when You were born, You were silent. "Human life should not be spent crying." Was this the message of your silence?

pavanane-ppōle ellām puṇarunnu
patitarkk-āśvāsam-ekunnu dēvī nī
parama-prēmam nirlōbham vitarunnu
paricōṭuṇmaye bōdhippicciṭunnu

Like a gentle breeze, You embrace everyone. O Goddess, You console and uplift the fallen. You shower the flowers of supreme love and show everyone the supreme truth.

sakala-vēdānta-sāram nī sanmayi!
amalē sañcita-puṇyam nin darśanam
iniyoru nūru janmam kazhiññālum
ivanor-ālambam nīyamba niścayam!

O pure existence, You are the essence of all the Vedas. O pure one, we can have Your darshan only because of merits from past lives. Even if I have another hundred lives, O Mother, You will be my sole refuge and strength.

lūtayil ninnu (Malayalam)

lūtayil ninnu nūl-enna-pōle
vēdiyil ninnu porikaḷ-pōle
ētoru jyōtirmayiyil ninnum
jātamāy kāṇum prapañcam-ellām

Like the web spun by the spider, like sparks emanating from the sacred fire-pit, this universe manifests as your glorious form.

ariyunnōrkk-uḷḷilum ariyāttōrkk-uḷḷilum
arivāy viḷaṅgunna caitanyamē
karayatta-bhaktiyāl maramārum hṛdayattil
niravārnna-kāntiyāy viriyunnu nī

You are pure consciousness, shining as knowledge in both the wise and the ignorant. In hearts that pray to You with pure devotion, You lift the veil of ignorance and reveal your matchless, enchanting beauty.

padamūnni nilkkuvān paṇipeṭṭ-izhayunna
śiśuvākum enne nī kāṇunnillē
karamonnu nīṭṭumō tuṇayenikk-ēkumō
kanivōṭu nīyonn-uyarttiṭumō?

Don't You see this helpless infant crawling and struggling to stand? Won't You stretch out your hands to help me? Won't You be merciful and lift me up?

māḍī tārī (Gujarati)

māḍī tārī nāknī nath
manē gamtī rē, ōhō
manē gamtī rē –
tējē tēnā caḷkē lōk

O Mother, I love your beautiful face. I want to see it again and again.

ō tārā... ō tārā... ō tārā...
ō tārā kapāḷnō cāndalō
manē gamtō rē, ōhō
manē gamtō rē - tē tō
mārē cāndnē sūraj

O Mother, I love the bindi on Your forehead. It is like the moon and sun to me.

māḍī tāruṅ mukhaḍuṅ rē
manē gamtuṅ rē, ōhō
manē gamtuṅ rē - hūṅ tō
jāu vārī vārī mā

O Mother, I love Your nose ring whose brilliance illumines all the worlds.

kē tārī... kē tārī... kē tārī...
kē tārī kalāīnā maṇkā
manē gamtā rē ōhō

manē gamtā rē - raṇkē
haiyāmā tē mārā

O Mother, I love the beads on Your wrists. I feel their sounds in my heart.

tārī – sāḍīnō pālav
manē gamtō rē, ōhō
manē gamtō rē – lūchē
āṅsu duḥkhīyānā

O Mother, I love the dust of Your feet that takes us across the ocean of sorrow.

kētārā... kētārā... kētārā...
kētārā pagnī pāyal
manē gamtī rē ōhō
manē gamtī rē - nācē
sahuṅ tēnā jhaṅkār mā

O Mother, I love the edge of Your sari that wipes the tears of the sorrowful.

mā tārā caraṇīraj
manē gamtī rē ōhō
manē gamtī rē – layī
jāyi bhavpār mā

O Mother, I love the anklets on Your feet. Everyone dances to the jingle of Your anklets.

maiyyājī huṇ mērā (Punjabi)

maiyyājī huṇ mērā bēḍā pār
tusāṅ hī lagāṇā
nayī calaṇā nayī calaṇā
nayī calaṇā kōī bahānā

O Mother, You have only to carry me across the ocean of samsara. Will not work. Will not work. No excuse will work this time.

janam janam rēyā mē viṣayā dā kīḍā
raj raj pōgē phervī milayā pīḍā
huṇ pujyā terē dar tē mā
nayī jāṇā nayī jāṇā
mē khālī hath nayī jāṇā

Since many, many births, I have lived like a worm immersed in sense objects. Indulging in sense pleasures returned only pain. Finally, I arrived at your door. I will not go. This time I will not leave empty-handed.

maiyyājī huṇ mērā
bēḍā pār
tusāṅ hī lagāṇā

O Mother, You have only to carry me across the ocean of samsara.

garab dē andar sī hardam kaiṅdā
aithō bār kadōṅ mainu mintā sī kardā
pher māyā nē mainu kēr lēyā
mā chaḍānā mā chaḍānā
es māyā tō chaḍānā

Inside the womb, I always pleaded, "Take me out of here." Then (after birth), maya enslaved me. Mother rescue me, Mother rescue me. Rescue me from this maya!

ō maiyyā kar dē bēḍā pār
mērā kar dē bēḍā pār

O Mother, You have only to carry me across the ocean of samsara.

mākhan cōr (Hindi)

mākhan cōr pyārē, nand kiśōrē
ḍōr ye dil kī khīṅcē tērī ōr
hō ḍhūṇḍē gōpiyāṅ tujhkō
hō ḍhūṇḍē rādhā tujhkō
bīt gayī rāt sārī hō gayī bhōr

Darling butter thief, Krishna, my heart is drawn to You. The gopis and Radha search for You. The night has passed by and dawn has come.

harē kṛṣṇā harē kṛṣṇā
harē kṛṣṇā harē kṛṣṇā

Glory to Krishna!

mākhan rakhā hai hamnē, tumhārē liyē
ēk hī prārtthanā hai, man hī man mēṅ
cūrālō tum sārā mākhan
yē mākhan hai hamārā man
man kō kar diyā hamnē, tujhe arpaṇ
har pal kartē haiṅ kānhā, tērā smaraṇ

We have saved butter for You. Our one prayer is that You steal it all. This butter is our hearts, which we have surrendered to You. Every moment, O Krishna, we think of You.

yamūnā taṭ par āō, hamārē liyē
ham kō nehlā dō tum, divya prēm sē
zarā muraḷī bajā dēnā
ō thōḍī rās racā lēnā
tērē caraṇōṅ mēṅ hō jāyē dhanya jīvan
jīv aur parmātmā kā, hō milan

Come to us on the banks of the Yamuna. Bathe us in your divine love and play your flute! Play the divine rasa (Krishna's divine dance)! May our lives be made worthy at your feet. May the individual be united with the Supreme.

manasā... cēyavē (Telugu)

manasā... cēyavē... smaraṇa... ammanu...
manasā cēyi samaraṇa ammanu
samaraṇa cēyi manasā

O mind, always remember Divine Mother.

dēha-śuddhatā vāk-śuddhatā
manaḥ-śuddhatā kāvālanṭē

To get purity in body, speech and thoughts, remember Divine Mother always.

rāga-dvēṣamu kāma-krōdhamu
sukha-duḥkhamu dāṭālanṭē

To overcome likes and dislikes, desires, anger, happiness and sorrow, remember Divine Mother always.

manaḥ-śāntiyu sama-dṛṣṭiyu
buddhi-śuddhiyu kāvālanṭē

To get peace of mind, equal vision, and purity of mind, remember Divine Mother always.

manasigē kaccikoḷuva āse (Kannada)

manasigē kaccikoḷuva āse
manasigē haccikoḷuva āse
atu itu endu itu atu endu
viṣayagaḷali kaḷedu hōgi
mithyege jōtu bīḷuva āse

The mind likes to take a bite (of everything). The mind likes to stick (to everything). The mind likes to run after this and that, and get lost in the world. The mind wants to cling to illusion.

manasē kāraṇa bandhanakū – ī
manasē kāraṇa namma mōkṣaprāptigū

The mind is the cause of both attachment and liberation.

kaṇḍakaṇḍa tiṇḍigaḷanu tinnuva āse
nenṭabanṭarige anṭi koḷḷuva āse

The mind likes to devour everything it sees and likes to stick to every human relationship.

keṭṭanenapanu melaku hākuva āse
rāga-dvēṣagaḷali kāla kaḷeyuva āse

The mind likes to chew the cud of bad memories and likes to waste time on attraction and aversion.

manasigē satyasaṅga nīḍu
manasanu tattvajote māḍu
manasē, mananava nī māḍu
amṛtānandamaya nīnāgu

Give the mind the company of Truth. Make noble principles the mind's companions. O mind, engage in contemplation and become the very bliss of immortality.

mānava janmavu (Kannada)

mānava janmavu mahatvadembuvā
satyavanaritukō hē manujā
mana bandantē naḍeyuta mereyuta
janmava vyartthava goḷisadiru

Human birth is of highest significance. Do not waste it on whims and fancies. O man, realise this truth.

dēhave rathavu manavē lagāmu
gyānēndriyagaḷe pañcāśvagaḷu
buddhiyē sārathi nī yajamāna
gyānadi ratha sanmārgadi sāgaḷi

Your body is like a chariot, your mind is the reigns. Your five organs of knowledge are the five driving horses. Your intellect is the charioteer and you are the owner. With Self-knowledge, let the chariot travel the righteous path.

parōpakāra dīnarasēvē
phalāpēkṣē illada karmagaḷā
gayyuta kṛṣṇana manadali smarisi
upāsisavana mahimeya pogaḷu

Help the needy. Serve the destitutes and do good actions without expectations (Karma Yoga). Fix your mind on Krishna and sing his glories.

yādavēndrana yadukula nandagōpana
yatijana prēma kṛṣṇana
yaśōda kandana nenē – hari hari

Forever remember the king of the Yadava clan, the supreme son of the Yadava dynasty. Lord Krishna, dear to the sages, Hari, who is Yashoda's child!

maṇi-māṇiku (Hindi)

maṇi-māṇiku yut svarṇa-kirīṭini
śūl rathāṅg gadādhanu dhāriṇi
śārad cānd sī jyōti bikhērti
nācti viśva-racāvani cētani

She wears a gem-studded gold crown and bears the trident and the mace. She spreads light like the autumn moon. Her dance creates the Universe. She is the embodiment of pure consciousness.

māt bhavāni simha-vāhani tīn lōk jananī
pāhi mahēśī pāpa-nāśinī tūhi duḥkh-haraṇī

Mother Bhavani rides a lion. Mother of the three worlds, destroyer of sins and sorrows, protect us.

jay mā... jay mā... jay mā... jay mā...
jay mā... jay mā... jay mā... jay mā...

Victory to Mother!

vidhimādhav gaurīś sarīkhē

sur-gaṇ-sārē śīṣ jhukhātē
has kē jab mahiṣāsur sirpē
nartan kartī māt bhavāni

Worshiped by Brahma, Vishnu and Shiva, adored by the gods, She dances the dance of destruction of the demon Mahishasura (ego).

sumirē mā sab satguṇ-śālini
jagdhātri jaya jag uddhāriṇi
duḥkh durit miṭ jāyē janani
jīvan jyōti jagē jan janmē

We meditate on the embodiment of Truth, Mother and saviour of the Universe. All sorrows vanish by your grace, and the flame of bliss lights up every heart.

manidā manidā (Tamil)

manidā manidā nī mayankāde
punidattai puriyāmal uzhalāte
unnil nī yārenḍru arivāyē
unnuḷḷē uṇmayai uṇarvāyē

O man, life is sacred. Do not waste your time and fall prey to delusion. Instead use your time to realize God. Know your Self. Realize the Truth within.

tavarizhaikka nēriḍunkāl iḍarāmal
tavamunikaḷ vazhankiṭṭa vēdāntam
karuttālē tannaiyē uṇarndiṭṭāḷ
karuttāgum vāzhvē punidamāgumē

Don't let circumstances confound you. Remember the Vedantic truths the sages uttered. If you realize the Self, your life becomes blessed.

māsadanai uḷḷamadil sērttiḍāmal
vēṣamadanai eḷitāka kaḷaindiḍalām
oḷirum siru dīpamalla kadiroḷiyē
ōmkāra pēruṇarvil kalandiḍuvāyē

If you don't let impurities clog your mind, you can easily shed identification with the body. You are not a candle to be lit. You are the self-effulgent Sun. Immerse yourself in the divine consciousness of Om.

veyil tāngi nizhaltarum maramāgi
mayakkattai teḷivikkum marundāki
iyarkkayil onḍriḍu arpaṇamāga
irai ninaivil niraindiḍu pūraṇamāga

Like a tree that gives shade from heat, like medicine that dispels drowsiness, surrender to God and become one with Nature. Be fulfilled by constantly remembering God.

maṇṇaiyaḷakka (Tamil)

maṇṇai aḷakka pōnāyō kaṇṇā kaṇṇā
viṇṇai aḷakka pōnāyō kaṇṇā kaṇṇā
veṇṇai tiruḍa pōnāyō kaṇṇā kaṇṇā – nī
ennai tiruḍa varuvāyō kaṇṇā kaṇṇā – nī
ennai tiruḍa varuvāyō kaṇṇā kaṇṇā

O Kanna, did you go to measure the earth? Or did you go to measure the sky? Or did you go to steal butter? Kanna, won't you come to steal my heart?

yaśōdaitān aḍittāḷō uralil kaṭṭi pōṭṭāḷō
arayil pūṭṭi vaittāḷō kaṇṇā kaṇṇā
maraikkum eṭṭā-poruḷ allavā kaṇṇā kaṇṇā – nī

maraikkum eṭṭā-poruḷ allavā kaṇṇā kaṇṇā

O Kanna, did mother Yashoda beat you? Or did she tie you to a mortar? Did she lock you in a room? But, Kanna aren't you beyond the reach of the scriptures?

dēvargaḷum pōttriḍavē yōgiyarum vāzhttiḍavē
rāsalīlai āḍuvadil kaṇṇā kaṇṇā
pāsattinai marandāyō kaṇṇā kaṇṇā – endan
pāsattinai marandāyō kaṇṇā kaṇṇā

O Kanna, with devas chanting and yogis praising, in the midst of dancing the Rasa leela, did you forget my love?

uṇmaiyāna anbu manam urugiḍumē pirivinilē
uṇmaiyinai kaṇḍariya kaṇṇā kaṇṇā
oḷindirundu pārkkirāyō kaṇṇā kaṇṇā – ennai
oḷindirundu pārkkirāyō kaṇṇā kaṇṇā

O Kanna, separation will melt a true loving heart. Are you hiding and watching me to see if that is true? Are you hiding and watching me to find out if that is true?

hē giridhāri kṛṣṇa murāri rādhikā ramaṇā
hē vanamāli kuñjavihāri mōhana vadanā
rādhe rādhe rādhe rādhe rādhe kṛṣṇa
rādhe rādhe rādhe rādhe rādhe kṛṣṇa

manōdarppaṇattil (Malayalam)

manō-darppaṇattil ennum ammē nin tiru-
vadanam
teḷiññonnu kāṇuvān ñān tapam-irippū

japiccum naltapiccum en vapussināl namiccum ñān
dinam-onnonnāy kozhiññu kāttirikkunnu

I ardently long to see Your holy face clearly in the mirror of my mind. I chant my mantra, perform austerities, and bow down with my whole body. Thus, days pass as I wait intently.

mizhikaḷil andhakāram paṭarnnu-pōy paṭavukaḷ
kaṭakkuvān kazhiyāte kuzhaññiṭumbōḷ
iruḷ-cūzhum vazhikaḷil uzhalum-en mizhikaḷil
oru ceru-tiri-nāḷam teḷikkuk-ammē... ammē teḷikkuk-ammē

Darkness shrouds my eyes. Unable to cross the river of life, I have become exhausted. I cannot see clearly in these darkened passageways. O Mother, please light a tiny lamp!

samsāra-pankam-ēttu iruḷ-āzhiyāy-en mana-
kara nīkkān karatāronn-aṇaccīṭēṇē
karaḷinte kayattil ninn-uyarunna kadanattin
cuzhiyil peṭṭulayāte karakēttaṇē... ammē karakēttaṇē

The dross of worldly life tarnishes my mind. Please help me remove the stains and draw me close to You. O Mother, please save me from drowning in the whirlpool of suffering deep within my heart.

prēma-payassil muṅgi kutirnnoren manatāril
padatārāl aṭivecconn-ezhunnaḷḷaṇē
kārakanna vānilindu mizhivārnnu nilkkumiva
marayākum-aham nīkki teḷiññiṭēṇē... ammē teḷiññiṭēṇē

Please let your holy footprints sanctify my heart, which is soaked in the milk of love. As dark clouds part to reveal the radiant moon, O Mother, please remove the veil of my ego and reveal Yourself.

man tō bandhi (Hindi)

man tō bandhi vahī purānā
tan kā kārāgār nayā
āśāyē tṛṣṇāyē vē hi
karmō kā sansār nayā

The mind is the same old prisoner. Only the prison of this body is new. Desires and thirsts are the same. Only the world etched by our karma is new.

vō hi mērā aham purānā
antar mērā rōj jalāyē
bhēd bhāv bhi vahī purānē
rūp nayē dhardhar kar āyē
vē hī sukh-duḥkh caltē man kō
bas unkā ādhār nayā
tan kā kārāgār nayā...
tan kā kārāgār nayā

The same old ego burns my being every day. My prejudices are the same, just clothed in new names. The same old pleasures and pains torture my mind. Only their forms are new. Only the prison of this body is new.

nisdin dēkhō prabhu kī līlā
karm bhūmi kā kṣētr nirālā
janm maraṇ kā cakr calākar

māyā mēṅ sabkō bharmāyā
sūtradhār tō pahcānā sā
nāṭak kā śṛṅgār nayā
tan kā kārāgār nayā
tan kā kārāgār nayā

Everyday, gaze at the Lord's divine play. This world of our karmas is so unique. By turning the wheel of birth and death, the Lord has ensnared us in the Great Illusion. The Director of this Play seems familiar. Only the decoration of the drama is new. Just the prison of this body is new.

manvā rē tu (Hindi)

manvā rē tu aisā thakā
na milā tujhē sukh kā patā
kahāṅ kahāṅ ḍūṇḍā tūnē usē
chipā hai kahāṅ, kiskō patā
manvā... rē... manvā... rē...

O man! You seem tired searching for happiness here and there. Where can you find happiness? No one can answer that, O man!

milā na kabhī vō mehalōṅ mēṅ
na cōṭī kē dhanvānō mēṅ
khōj rahē haiṅ vō bhī usē
kisi kē bhī jāl mēṅ, vō nā phasē
manvā... rē... manvā... rē...

You don't find it in palatial homes. Not among the richest of the rich. Even they search for it frantically. It is very difficult to obtain, O man!

sant vāṇī gūñjē man mē

ulaṭ nayan kō bhītar rē
sukh hai kahāṅ, viṣayōṅ mēṅ basā
uskā srōt hai andar rē
manvā... rē... manvā... rē...

The words of the sages resonate in the mind telling us to turn our eyes inwards. Happiness is not in sense objects. The essence of it is within, O man!

sukh kā sūraj ḍhaltā nahīṅ
uskā kōyī ant nahīṅ
gyān kī dṛṣṭi jaisē khulē
ānand dhan banē jīvan rē
manvā... rē... manvā... rē...

The sun of happiness never sets. True happiness is endless. When the eyes of true knowledge open, life is enriched with the wealth of happiness O man!

mā ō mā mārī (Gujarati)

mā ō mā mārī tuṅ mā
tārā sivā nathī kōī mārūṅ
kē tārā sivā nā jōvē kōī bījuṅ

O Mother, you are my mother. I have no one other than you, nor do I want anyone else.

tuṅ mārī sāthī tuṅ saṅgāthī
tu mārā śvāsōnā śvāsōśvās
rōm rōm mā tārō vās
kyārē samāviś mujhnē tujh mā...

You are my friend and companion. You are every breath I take. You live in every particle of my body. When will you let me merge in you?

tāruṅ māruṅ kēvuṅ ā bandhan
tuṅ mārī pāsē huṅ tārāthī dūr
huṅ ātmā tuṅ paramātmā
kyārē samāviś mujhnē tujh mā...

O Mother, what kind of attachment is this? You are so close yet I feel so far away from you. When will you let me merge in you?

tu mārī dēvī ā jagnī tu jananī
tārā caraṇō mā cārō lōk
huṅ ā jagmā ā jag tuj mā
kyārē samāviś mujhnē tujh mā...

O Mother, You are my Goddess. You are the Mother of this world. All worlds are at your feet. I belong to this world, and this world belongs to you.

maraṇattin-oru cuvaṭu (Malayalam)

maraṇattin-oru cuvaṭu-arikattil-eppōzhum
manujā nin janmam-enn-ariyēṇam-innu nī
oru noṭi matiyatu poliyuvān kumiḷapōl
gatakāla jaladhiyil smṛtiyāyi marayuvān
varuvānuḷḷ-oru kālam mati-tande varutiyil
karutalāy-illennu ariyēṇam-innu nī
ciramāyi nilakoḷḷum śivarūpa-bhajanam tān
citamāyat-atu mātram ariyēṇam-innu nī
ōm namaḥ śivāya ōm namaḥ śivāya

O Man, know that every moment, takes you one step closer to death. Life can end at any moment, and like a bubble, the remaining memories will sink in the waters of the past. Realize that your intellect cannot control the future. Know that the worship of Lord Shiva, the eternal Truth, is the one auspicious and essential deed to perform in your life.

paralōka-narakatte veṭiyunna sukṛtamāy
janiyārnna putrande cita-nōkki-nilppavar
iha-lōka-vāridhi naṭuvilāy nilppavar
imayonnu cimmiyāl iniyent-ariyāttōr
uyirārnna noṭimutal nizhalāyi tuṭarunna
poruḷitu maraṇam-enn-ariyēṇam-innu nī
ciramāyi nilakoḷḷum śivarūpa-bhajanam tān
citamāyat-atu mātram ariyēṇam-innu nī
ōm namaḥ śivāya ōm namaḥ śivāya

Desolate parents stand beside the funeral pyre of their son, lamenting the one gone before his time. Many stand lost in the vast ocean of life, unsure of their next moment. The only certainty for everyone is death. It shadows them from birth itself. The worship of Lord Shiva, the eternal Truth, is the one auspicious and essential deed to perform in your life.

jani-ārnna noṭiyil mṛtiy-ārnnu palatum
ariyāte nām vṛthā ciriyārnnitannē
pakal-onnu varumeṅkil iruvuṇḍu pinnil
uyiriṅgitārnnāl mṛtiyuṇḍ-itoppam
kozhiyunna nimiṣaṅgaḷ nitarām avaniyil
ninavāṇu vāzhvennum ariyēṇam-innu nī
ciramāyi nilakoḷḷum śivarūpa-bhajanam tān
citamāyat-atu mātram ariyēṇam-innu nī
ōm namaḥ śivāya ōm namaḥ śivāya

In the moment of our birth, death has come to many others; oblivious of this, we rejoice. Night follows day. Likewise, when we take birth, death comes along with us. Moments on this Earth not spent in the remembrance of the Lord are wasted. Know that the worship of Lord Shiva, the eternal Truth, is the one auspicious and essential deed to perform in your life.

mārgamulu enni (Telugu)

mārgamulu enni unna gamyamokkaṭē – vipra
bhāṣyamulu enni unna satyamokkaṭē
ī nijamu palikēdi sanātana dharmamu telusuko
ēkam sat viprā bahudā vadanti

Though there are many paths, the destination is one. Though there are diverse scholarly commentaries, the Reality is one. Sanatana Dharma reveals this truth. Truth is One. The wise call it by different names.

samskāramunu baṭṭi mārgamu ceppiri
ṛṣulu kramarītulatō dārulu cūpiri
sarvamu brahmamayam nīvu-nēnu daivamanē
darśana jīvanamē sanātana dharmamu

Diverse paths were created to accommodate diverse temperaments. Seers gave us different spiritual practices to suit different temperaments. Everything is divine, including you and I. Perceiving this Truth, every moment is the essence of Sanatana Dharma.

mukkōṭi dēvatalu ṣanmatamulu pūjalu
vēda-vēdāṅgamulu āru-darśanamulu
bhakti jñāna rāja karma yōga mārgamulu
sarva samanvayamē sanātana dharmamu

Sanātana Dharma encompasses 30 million deities, six religious divisions, numerous rituals, the Vedas and their auxiliary branches, and six schools of philosophy, as well as the yogic paths of devotion, knowledge, meditation and action. Sanātana Dharma harmonizes all disparate paths and philosophies.

māye tanna (Kannada)

māye tanna pāśadinda
jagava suttu tiruvaḷu
janara ādisu tiruvaḷu
jagava ādisu tiruvaḷu

Maya entangles the world with her noose. She makes people play as she wants. She makes the world play as she wants.

dēvi dayāmayiyu sadā
jagava suttu tiruvaḷu
māyā pāśava biḍisi ada
hindake sutti koḷuvaḷu
hindake sutti koḷuvaḷu

Merciful Devi goes around the world, undoing the noose of maya, and rewinding it.

dayāmayi dēvi mahāmāye dēvi

O merciful Devi, you are more than Maya.

kāṇada daiva nambevemba
ādhunika janara munde
kōṭi raviya tējadi
dēvi śobhisu tiruvaḷu

dēvi śobhisu tiruvaḷu

Before the modern generation who say they can't believe in invisible God, Devi shines like a million suns.

tanna prēma nūlininda
namma pōṇisi koḷuvaḷu
karuṇeyinda koraḷa hāra
hṛdaya kānisi koḷuvaḷu
hṛdaya kānisi koḷuvaḷu

She strings us as beads in her love mala and compassionately presses that mala to her heart.

mērī dēvīmā (Punjabi)

mērī dēvīmā āyī hai aj
mērī dēvīmā āyī hai aj
lakkhāṅ khuṣiyāṅ nū leykē
śubhkaḍī huṇ āyīhē aj
śubhkaḍī huṇ āyīhē aj

The divine Mother arrived today, bringing lots of happiness. The divine Mother arrived today.

māyātōṅ laijāṇ pār
mērī dēvīmā āyi hai aj
mērī dēvīmā āyi hai aj

To take us across this ocean of maya, the divine Mother arrived today.

satraṅkī mālā... ambar vicc
basanti phullādī... harthā mehek

lakkhāṅ sūrajdī camak leykē... hoy
jagan-mayīmā āyī hai aj
jagan-mayīmā āyī hai aj

A rainbow-colored garland in the sky and the fragrance of spring flowers all around, the Mother of the Universe arrived today with the radiance of millions of suns.

mērī dēvīmā āyi hai aj
mērī dēvīmā āyi hai aj

My divine Mother arrived today.

nīliyā hai akkhāṅ kuṅkurālē vāl
mōtiyādī muskān sirtē tāj
amṛt tārādī varkhāṅ kardī... hoy
śērāvālīmā āyi hai aj
śērāvālīmā āyi hai aj

With beautiful eyes, curly hair, a pearl-like smile, and a crown on Her head, She showers the divine nectar of eternal bliss.

maiyā dī jaykār (jayjaykār bulāvō nāl)
jō palpal sāḍēnāl (jayjaykār bulāvō nāl)
asīsādā darbār (jayjaykār bulāvō nāl)
khuśiyā dī jhaṅkār (jayjaykār bulāvō nāl)

Victory to the divine mother, the One who is always with us. (Call out "Victory to the divine Mother!") One with abundant Grace, One who is an explosion of happiness (call out "Victory to the divine Mother!")

mōr paṅkh (Hindi)

mōr paṅkh sir pē suhānā... hōy hōy hōy hōy

cānd sā hē sundar cēharā
rūp mānas mēṅ hō tērā
mākhan cōrā citt cōrā
rādhē śyām gōpī śyām kānhā... hōy hōy hōy hōy
rādhē śyām gōpī śyām kānhā

A beautiful peacock feather adorns Your hair, O Krishna. Your face is more beautiful than the moon. May Your lovely form ever shine in my heart. May Your lovely form ever shine in my heart. Butter thief, You captivate my mind. O Shyam, You are the beloved of Radha and the gopis (milkmaids).

bōlē śyām bōlē śyām rādhē rādhē śyām
bōlē śyām bōlē śyām rādhē rādhē śyām
rādhē rādhē rādhē rādhē rādhē ghana śyām
rādhē ghana śyām

Let us chant "Shyam Radhe Shyam!" O Beloved of Radha, Shyam, Your dark skin is the color of monsoon clouds.

virah pūrṇimā cāndini rāt mēṅ
prēm rūp rākēndu jyōt mēṅ
rās nāc mēṅ śyām kē hāth lē
gōpiyāṅ sabhī nāctī jōṣ mēṅ

On this full-moon night, I feel my separation from You intensely. In this splendid moonlight, I bask in Your love. Holding Krishna's hand, all the gopis gladly joined the rasa dance (the Lord's divine dance).

vēṇugān kī mādhuri phail gayī
śyām rūp mēṅ līn hai sabhī
rās kēli kē nāc mēṅ rādhikā
śyām samān hō gayī sāṅvalī

The sweet melodies of His divine flute spread everywhere, enchanting all. Krishna's beloved Radhika was so absorbed in the divine dance that her very complexion became dark like the Lord's.

mukiloḷi niram (Malayalam)

mukiloḷi niram-ārnnavan – avan
hṛdaya muraḷika mīṭṭuvōn
viralil giriyey-uyarttavan – avan
koṭiya kāḷiya marddakan

His colour is like the rain-cloud and he plays the flute of the heart. He lifted the mountain with his finger, and defeated Kaliya, the ferocious snake.

harē kṛṣṇa... harē kṛṣṇa...

vraja-vadhū-jana nāyakan – avan
akhila-bhuvana vidhāyakan
naḷina-nayana manōharan – avan
yadu-kulōttama kēśavan

He is the leader of gopis, and the ruler of all the worlds. His lotus eyes capture the mind. He is Keshava, the most excellent one of the Yadu race.

muraharē jaya mādhavā – śrita
śaraṇa-dāyaka śrīdharā
caraṇa-naḷina yugattil-aṭiyanu
śaraṇam-ēkaṇamē – sadā

O Slayer of the demon Mura, victory to Madhava, the one who gives refuge. O consort of Lakshmi! Always grant me refuge at Your lotus feet.

akhila-guṇa-gaṇa samyutan – avan
anagha-mānasa pūjitan
atiśayātmaka vaibhavan – avan
amṛta-rūpan-adhōkṣajan

Complete with all the noble qualities, He is worshipped by the pure-minded. His glory is wondrous. He is Adhokshajan who is eternal and who transcends the senses.

natajanārtti vināśakan – avan
haraviriñca suvanditan
madhuratan maṇi-dīpamām – avan
avanibhāram-akattiyōn

He destroys the devotees' sorrows and is worshipped by Shiva and Brahma. He is the glorious lamp of Mathura, and He destroyed evil on Earth.

koṭiya saṅgara bhūmiyil – avan
naranu sārathiyāyavan
yōgakārakan-avyayan – avan
yōgivṛnda niṣēvitan

He drove Arjuna's chariot on the ferocious battlefield. He is the eternal One ever established in yoga, and is served by all the yogis.

jñāna-gītayatōtiyōn – avan
jñāna-rūpan-anāmayan
sujanapālana tatparan – avan
śrutisusāra parātparan

The embodiment of wisdom and free of all afflictions, He instructed the Gita. Eager to protect good people, He is the true essence of the Vedas, the Supreme One.

muttu muttu māriyamma (Tamil)

muttu muttu māriyamma
muttazhagi dēviyamma
muttamizhāl vāzhttukindrōm
mūvulakum pōttriḍavē
muttēvarum vaṇankiḍum dēviyamma
muttēviyē ōmkāriyē kāḷiyamma

O Mariyamma, beautiful Goddess! The three worlds praise You through poetry, music and drama. You are Parvati, Lakshmi, Sarasvati and Kali. You are also the embodiment of Om. Brahma, Vishnu and Shiva worship You.

īndra tāyē makkaḷai manatil vaikinḍrāy
iniyavaḷē akhilattai uḷ niraikkindrāy
inbattilum tunbattilum unnai pōttriḍavē
inidāna pērinba vāzhvu taruvāyē

O Mother, You cherish us in Your heart. You pervade the entire universe. We worship You in pleasure and pain. Please bless us with a blissful life.

aruḷāṭci seybavaḷē manasākṣi āgindrāy
avaniyilē anbum amaidiyum pozhigindrāy
manadil vaittēn unnai karuttil vaittēn
vinai tīrkka valam varum selviyamma

You govern the universe with compassion. You are indeed my conscience. You shower love and peace on earth. I cherish You always. You travel the world removing the karma of Your children.

kāḷīśvari vāgīśvari nādēśvari śaraṇam
lōkēśvari māhēśvari nāgēśvari śaraṇam

ōmkāri aimkāri hrīmkāri śaraṇam
kāḷi triśūli rājarājēśvari śaraṇam

I take refuge in You, O Kali. O Goddess of speech, music and the world, I take refuge in You. O Supreme Goddess and Goddess of Nagas, You are the embodiment of the Bijaaksharas—Om, Aim and Hrim. O Kali, O Supreme Empress, I take refuge in You!

kāḷī śaraṇam lakṣmī śaraṇam durgē śaraṇam
dēvī śaraṇam bhadrē śaraṇam rudrē śaraṇam

O embodiment of Kali, Lakshmi, Durga, Devi, Bhadrā and Rudrā, I take refuge in You!

nācē kānuḍō nācē (Gujarati)

nācē kānuḍō nācē
tā... tātāthaiyā tā... tātāthaiyā tāthaiyā
nācē kānuḍō nācē
tātāthaiyā tātāthaiyā tātāthaiyā tā... thaiyā

Baby Krishna is dancing!

nānā nānā caraṇ tēnā
caraṇē bāndhī jhāñjar jhīṇī
nānī nānī paglī bharī nācē...

With tiny anklets tied on His tiny feet, taking tiny steps, Baby Krishna is dancing.

nāthyō tēṇē kāliyānē
kāliyō bhaythi thar tharē
kāliyānī māthē caḍī nācē

Baby Krishna conquered the serpent Kaliya who shivered with fear as Baby Krishna climbed up on his hood and danced.

līlā tēni kēvī jūō
jagnē nacāvanārō
nācē bhaktōnā dīlmā nācē

Look at His lilas. The One who makes the world dance, dances in the hearts of His devotees. Baby Krishna is dancing.

bhaktimā bhān bhūlī... nācē nācē
bhaktōnā dilmā kānō... nācē nācē
jay kanhaiyā lāl bōlō... nācē nācē
jay kāliyā mardan... nācē nācē

Everyone is dancing, forgetting themselves in devotion. Kanna dances in the hearts of his devotees. Little Kanna is dancing. The slayer of Kaliya is dancing! Forgetting themselves in devotion, everyone is dancing. In the heart of His devotees Baby Krishna is dancing. Victory to Krishna, Victory to the conqueror of the serpent Kaliya.

nācē nācē kānō nācē nācē

Krishna is dancing!

nandalālā yadu nandalālā (Hindi)

nandalālā yadu nandalālā
vṛndāvana gōvinda bālā
rādhālōlā nandalālā
rādhā mādhava nandalālā

O Beloved son of Nanda, enchanting little Lord of Vrindavan, Beloved of Radha.

hari hari hari hari smaraṇ karō
hari caraṇ kamal dhyān karō
muralī mōhan naman karō
giridhar murahar bhajan karō
giridhar murahar bhajan karō

Remember the name of Hari (Krishna). Meditate on His Lotus Feet. Bow to the bearer of the Divine Flute. Sing the glories of Giridhara, the Lord who bears our mountain of worries effortlessly when we surrender to Him.

madhur madhur muraḷidhara śyāmā
mathurādhipatē rādhē śyāmā
sūrdās prabhu hē giridhāri
mīrā kē prabhu hṛdaya vihāri
mīrā kē prabhu hṛdaya vihāri

O Sweet Lord Shyam, Lord of Mathura, Beloved of Radha. The Lord worshipped by the great saint Surdas. The Lord who ever resided in the heart of Meera, the greatest of devotees.

rādhē rādhē rādhē rādhē rādhē gōvindā
rādhē gōvindā
vṛndāvana canda kandā mukundā
anandā mukundā

Chant the names of Lord Krishna. The beautiful darling Krishna, the giver of freedom.

narajanmōgu (Tulu)

narajanmōgu battibokka ullā nama nālayn
dinokku

ātu dina malpuga ammana pādāsēvenu... ammana pādāsēvenu

A human life lasts for just a few days. Let us spend that precious time serving Mother.

bannaga kāsu kaniyērē ijji pōnagalā koniyērē ijji
lōka panpina śāśvata attu dharma mārgōnu buḍupina atta
hṛdayāndhakārōnu gettudu ātmatatvōnu bōdhane maltudu
vivēka vairāgyōnu korle māyānāśini... dēvi bandhamōcini

We bring no money with us when we come. We take nothing with us when we go. As we walk the path of dharma (righteousness), let us remember that nothing in this world is eternal. O Dispeller of Delusion, bestow on me discernment and dispassion. O Goddess, You release us from all bondage.

kāmini kāñcaṇa āse dīdu āsti baduku bōḍu paṇḍudu
sukha duḥkha māyōḍu būrdu aleyondullā aleyondullā
nīrda mittu itti guḷḷe yētu kāla uppuṇḍu panlē
ī satyōnu nenetu badukarē sāditojālē... dēvi hṛdinivāsini

Lust and greed enslave us. We hoard money and property. Falling prey to the spell of pleasure and grief, we wander around aimlessly. Like bubbles on the water's surface, life is ephemeral. Help us remember this truth and show us how to live. O Goddess, You dwell in our hearts.

suguṇa manōhari śivaramaṇi
gauri manōhari jagajanani

O consort of Lord Śiva, You are noble in character. O Mother of the universe, You captivate all hearts.

navvu navvu (Telugu)

navvu navvu navvu... ēḍupu āpi navvu
amma navvamandi... amma navvamandi

Smile, smile, smile... Stop crying and smile! Mother asks us to smile. She asks us to laugh.

sommulenni vunna, padavulenni vunna
mandi enta vunna, nī āśalēnni tīru
puṭṭinōḍu cāvunu, caccinōḍu puṭṭunu
puṭṭi ēḍci cacci ēḍci ēla ēḍcē bratuku

Regardless of your wealth, or the number of your titles, or the number of people around you, how many of your desires are fulfilled? Who is born must die. Who dies is born again. We cry at birth. We cry when dying. Why cry throughout life?

amma navvamandi ahaha hahaha
amma navvamandi ohoho hohoho

Mother asks us to laugh, aha ha ha. Mother asks us to laugh, oho ho ho.

endaru enni annā... okka navvu navvu
krinda jāri paḍinā... paiki lēci navvu
ēnni bādhalunnā... maraci marala navvu
gāli pīlci, gālivadili – navvi navvi bratuku

Many may blame you—give a laugh. You may stumble and fall. Get up and laugh. You may face many problems. Forget them and smile. While breathing in and out, laugh! Live life filled with laughter!

amma vundi antā, manakū ēla cinta
amma vundi tōḍu, bhayamu lēka navvu
nuvvu navvu tuṇṭē sṛṣṭi navvutundi
amma navvu cūsicūsi, āḍi pāḍi navvu

Mother is everywhere. So why worry? Mother is with us all the time. So drop your fears and smile. When you smile, the whole creation will smile. Look at Mother's smile, and dance and smile and laugh!

nēh mujhē dō (Hindi)

nēh mujhē dō... nij caraṇōṅ kā
ab tō rahā na jāyē
virah agnī mēṅ bhasm hō rahā
mukh sē kahā na jāyē
mukh sē kahā na jāyē
mukh sē kahā na jāyē

Grant me love to your feet. I can no longer bear this. The fire of separation is burning me to ashes. And I can't describe my state.

mērā man hī mērā duśman
viṣayōṅ mēṅ bhaṭkāyē
dūjī tērī sundar māyā
barbas darmāyē rōg
baḍā hai ab tō itnā
dard sahā na jāyē

My mind is my enemy that constantly distracts me with the objects of the world. And then Your beautiful illusory Power forcefully deludes me. The disease is now so severe that the pain is unbearable.

tumnē bhējā amarit dēkar
mainē viṣ apnāyā
kṣaṇ-bhaṅgur tan par mōhit hō
amar lōk visarāya duḥkh
dētā mujhkō bhavsāgar
ab tō bahā na jāyē

You sent me the nectar of immortality but I preferred poison. Deluded and bewitched by the perishable body, I forgot the world of immortality. This ocean of transmigration gives nothing but sorrow. And now I am drowning.

nel tarum (Tamil)

nel tarum mutteḍuttu uṇavākkalām – ammā
nīr tarum mutteḍuttu saram kōrkkalām
soltarum mutteḍuttu kaviyākkalām unadu
sēvai tarum muttukk-edai nigar-ākkalām

The paddy rice can make food. The ocean pearl can make a garland. The best words can make a poem. Mother, nothing is more precious than the bliss of doing your seva.

annaitarum muttadanil anbinai peralām
tandai tarum muttadanil paṇbinai peralām
āsānin muttadanil arivinai peralām
ammā un muttattilō anaittaiyum peralām
ammā un muttattilō anaittaiyum peralām

Mother gives us the pearl of love. Father gives us the pearl of good character. Teacher gives us the pearl of knowledge. Mother gives us everything.

uttravarin muttadanil urutuṇai uṇḍu
uravinarin muttadanil ūkkamum uṇḍu
anbargaḷin muttadanil ārudal uṇḍu
ammā un muttam-adarkku īṭiṇaiyuṇḍō?
ammā un muttam-adarkku īṭiṇaiyuṇḍō?

A friend can give us the pearl of support. A relative can give us the pearl of encouragement. A loved one can give us the pearl of comfort. Mother, nothing can equal your precious kiss.

nī viral toṭṭāl (Malayalam)

nī viral toṭṭāl pāṭunna vīṇayām
ī janmam saphalam enn-ammē
nin mozhi kēlkkān kātōrtt-irikkayāṇu
ī dhanya bhūmiyil ammē

O Mother! The veena of my life attains fulfillment when it sings at the touch of your fingers. I wait with longing on this blessed earth to hear your melodious voice.

tāmara-ppūvitaḷ tumbile tēn-kaṇam
vāri-eṭukkum vasanta-rāvil
maññin kaṇaṅgaḷ pōl ārdramāy jīvanil
snēhāmṛtam tūki nilkkum ammē
nī-ende saṅgīta rāga-vṛndam – ammē
nī-ende ātmāvin śānti-mantram

Mother, on this night, when spring scoops honey dew from the tips of the lotus petals, You fall as gently as snow upon me. You shower the ambrosia of love in my life. O Mother! You are every melody within me and you are my mantra of peace.

mārivil gōpuram māṭi viḷikkavē
tāraṅgaḷ-ālōlam āṭi nilkke
manvantaraṅgaḷāy ī śyāma vāṭiyil
ānanda gītamāy vannor-ammē
nī-ende vāṭiyil dēva-tāram – ammē
nī-ende kōvilil dēva-śilpam

Up in the sky, the rainbow beckons You, and the stars wait in anticipation. O Mother! In all the ages, You have come to earth as the song of infinite bliss. You are the divine star in my garden. You are the divine idol enshrined in the temple of my heart.

nīlāñjana mizhi (Kannada version)

nīlāñjana nētra nīrada varṇā
nīnē gati yenagendu kṛṣṇā
husiyallā prabhu nīnē gatiyu
ēkādhāra nī kṛṣṇā

bālakumārana līlegaḷāḍuve
śyāmala kōmala kṛṣṇā
nārada tumburu nādapriyane
mānasa mōhana kṛṣṇā

kīrtana nartana ārtivināśana
śāśvata bhāsura kṛṣṇā
ēṣaṇa nīguva vīkṣaṇe nīḍu

sākṣibhāvātmaka kṛṣṇā

māyāmōhana mānava sēvita
pāda sarōjā kṛṣṇā
bhūtala vāsadi biḍugaḍe nīḍu
mōkṣapradāyaka kṛṣṇā

nīlō nīlō nīlōnē (Telugu)

nīlō nīlō nīlōnē
antā unnadi nīlōnē
śivuḍu unnadi nīlōnē
nīlōnē... nīlōnē...

Within you, within you, within You, everything is within you. Even Shiva is within you. Within you, within you

sṛṣṭiki artthamu nīlōnē
rūpapu bimbamu nīlōnē
śabdamu gamyamu nīlōnē
sparśaku sphuraṇa nīlōnē

Creation occurs within you. Forms (that you see) are a reflection within you. Sound ends within you. Response to touch happens within you.

rāgamu dvēṣamu nīlōnē
bandhamu mōkṣamu nīlōnē
śivuni vetakāli nīlōnē
nēnanu eruka śivuḍēlē

Likes and dislikes happen within you. Bondage and liberation are within you. Search Shiva within you. "I am" awareness within is Shiva alone.

jaya jaya śankara hara hara śankara
śiva śiva śankara śambhō śankara

ninna naguvu (Kannada)

ninna naguvu pasariside ellarā hṛdayadalli
prēma nīḍi namma manava parivartiside amma
makkaḷannu uddharisalu avatariside jagadoḷu
jaganmāteyāgi nī beḷagutihe amma

Your beautiful smile falls as all-showering Love. You have changed our hearts, O Mother. You have incarnated on this earth to uplift Your children. O Mother Kali, You shine as the Mother of the Universe.

amma jaganmātē dēvī kāḷī mātē
amma jaganmātē dēvī kāḷi mātēmalligeya
sugandhavu ninna sānniddhya ammā

ninna darśana paḍeyalu bandiheyu amma
arivillada ninna makkaḷa kāpāḍu ammā
nīnobbaḷe namagāśraya hē dayā sindhu

Fragrant as jasmine is Your Presence. We have come for Your Divine Darshan. Please protect your ignorant children. You are our only refuge, O Compassionate One, O Mother Kali.

sat cintanadalli namma magnagoḷisu tāyē
mōha pāśava biḍisi dharma mārgava bōdhisu
namma manadalli ninna caraṇa kamala
ajñāna kaḷedu muktiya prasādisu

Bless us to think only good thoughts. And extricate us from the bonds of attachment. Teach us the path of Dharma (the Eternal Truth). May Your Sacred Feet rest ever in our hearts. Rid us of ignorance and bless us with Freedom, O Mother Kali.

ninna nirmala (Kannada)

ninna nirmala prēmake paravaśanādē
enna manadi divya jyōti beḷagamma

I surrender to your pure unconditional love. Please light the divine lamp in my mind.

enna bāḷige nī beḷakāgi bande
ninnusire ī jagada prāṇavamma
śraddhē bhakti viśvāsava dayapālisi
enna janmava sārthaka goḷisamma
ammā... ammā... ammā... ennammā...

You came as light in my life. Your breath sustains the life force of this world. Please bestow faith and devotion in me. Please make my life useful to others, O Mother.

parara kaṣṭagaḷanariyuva śakti nīḍamma
enna karagaḷa sad viniyōga vāgali
enna kāryavella nissvārtha sēveyāgali
jagadi elleḍe sukha śānti nelesali
ammā... ammā... ammā... ennammā...

Please grant me strength to understand the difficulties of others. Let my hands be used for auspicious purposes. Let all my deeds be selfless service. Let peace be throughout the universe

ellarallu ninna kāṇuva dṛṣṭi nīḍu

ahaṅkāra tolagisi śaraṇāgati nīḍu
jñāna siddhi kṛpe gaidu ajñānava aḷisu
ninna caraṇa kamalagaḷe enagāśraya
ammā... ammā... ammā... ennammā...

Please bless me to see You in others. Kindly bless me to shed my ego and grant me intellect to surrender to you. Please have mercy and bestow knowledge to remove my ignorance. Your lotus feet are my refuge.

ninu kīrtimpa (Telugu)

ninu kīrtimpa mañci hṛdayamēdi
nī kīrttana pāḍa mañci bhāvamu ēdi

Where is the good heart in me, to adore your greatness? Where are the good feelings in me, to sing your bhajans?

kalmaṣa vāsanatō madi ceḍutunnadi
bhāvaśuddhi lēka bhakti vīgucunnadi
japamu lēka manassu jārutunnadi
vividha karmala naḍuma naligi pōtunnadi
ammā... ammā... ammā... ammā

My mind has degenerated due to impure thoughts. Without pure thoughts (within), my devotion shrivels and dries up. Unable to do japa, my mind slips away. My mind gets trampled in the vortex of many actions, O Mother.

ammā... nā mora ālakimpavā ammā
prēma viśvāsa-bhakti nā centalēvamma
bhakti bhikṣamunicci kāpāḍavā amma
prēma hṛdayamicci rakṣimpavā ammā

ammā... ammā... ammā... ammā

O mother, please hear my cry. I feel no love, no devotion, no faith. Please fill my heart with love and devotion. Please protect me.

śaṅkari śaraṇam janani śaraṇam śaraṇamu jagadamba
pārvati śaraṇam mahēṣi śaraṇam śaraṇamu jagadamba

O Auspicious Mother of the universe, I take refuge in You. O Parvati, O Empress, O universal Mother, I take refuge in You.

niścala koḷada (Kannada)

niścala koḷada nirmala jaladi
nā ninna kaṇḍukoṇḍe
hṛdaya kamalada mēlondu dhavaḷa
śankhuvinante beḷagiruvē

In the still pond, on its pure water, I beheld You. In the heart lotus, You shine like a white conch.

stabdha niśabda citrada teradi
siddhavāgali dhyāna
bāleya manake balavilla amma
olumeyindī kṣaṇa hiḍidiḍu nī

May my meditation be perfect, like a still and silent picture. O Mother, this child's mind is too weak. Please hold this moment with love.

ondē bēḍikē dēviye kēḷu
ādhivyādhigaḷa nīgisu

īkṣaṇavē terē anantateya tere
nirantaravāgali anubhūti

O Devi, please listen to my prayer. May problems and pain not bother me. Please remove the curtain that veils Eternity. May the experience of the divine remain at all times.

nit din tarsē (Hindi)

nit din tarsē nain hamārē
darśan dījō kṛṣṇa murārē
vṛndāvan kē mōhan pyārē
nand yaśōdā kē bāl dulārē

O Krishna, our eyes constantly yearn to see You. Most beloved of Vrindavan, you are the apple of Nanda's and Yaśōda's eyes.

man kē jharōkhōṅ sē tujhē hi dēkhuṅ
rāt aur din bas tujhē hi pūjuṅ
har kṣaṇ har pal tērā guṇ gāvūṅ
aisā var dē dō manamōhan tum

Through the windows of my mind, I see only Your form. I worship You day and night. Please grant me the boon of singing Your praises every moment.

hē śyām gōpālā! hē manamōhanā!

O Śyām (dark-hued one)! O Gōpāla (protector of cows)! O Manamōhana (enchanter of hearts)!

tērē cintan mēṅ bitāvūṅ yē jīvan
sauṅpu tujhē maiṅ apnā tan man
har karm karuṅ tujhkō samarppaṇ

vinati sunlē hamāri tu mōhan

May I spend my whole life remembering You. May I surrender my body, mind and actions to You. O Krishna, please fulfill this prayer!

nṛttamāḍu (Malayalam)

nṛttamāḍu nṛttamāḍu nṛttamāḍu bālakā
nṛttamāḍu nṛttamāḍu nṛttamāḍu bālakā

Dance, dance, dance, O young boy! dance, dance, dance.

dhim dhimidhimi dhim dhimidhimi
mēgha carmma ghōṣamō
vānil ninnum dēvakaḷ
muzhakkiṭunna vādyamō
ugra-darppam-ēntiṭunnu
kāḷiyande pattiyil
indracāpam-ēnti-nilkkum
anti mēgham-ennapōl

The rhythm of your steps is like the drumming of thunder clouds. Or is it the drum beats of the celestial beings in the sky upon the hood of Kaliya, the fiercely proud and poisonous snake. Krishna, You appear as a dark cloud holding the shimmering rainbow.

mālya kankaṇādikaḷ
karṇṇa bhūṣayābhakaḷ
sūrya śōbha maṅgiyō
minnalonnu cimmiyō
dig gajaṅgaḷ-uddhyatam
utirtta nāda-ghōṣamō

uragamonnuṭal piṇaccu
cīriyārtta nādamō

You are adorned with tinkling ornaments—garlands, bangles and earrings. The brilliance of the sun dims, and lightning fades compared with your splendor. Are the eight elephants holding the eight directions trumpeting in joy? Is it your ringing laughter as you dance on the intertwining hoods of the snake?

pīlinīrtti āṭiṭunna
kēki tande cēloṭu
sarppa śīrṣa maṇḍalattil
nṛtta vēgam-ārnniṭum
āzhiyārnna vantira
onnuyarnna marnna pōl
kāḷa sarppa śīrṣavum
ijjalattil-āzhnnuvō

With the beauty of a dancing peacock, fanning its colorful feathers, your dance gains momentum on the circle of the snake's hoods. Like a huge ocean wave, swelling and subsiding, the hood of the deadly snake sank deep into the waters.

mandharādri sindhuvil
ennapōl patikkayō
uraga dēhamākavē
cēvaṭikku cūzheyāy
rājamalli pūttulañña
māmalayakku nēritā
śōṇitattil muṅgiyārttu
kēṇiṭunnu kāḷiyan

It was as if the huge Mandara mountain had crashed into the ocean. The snake sank deep beneath His dancing feet. The Lord resembled a beautiful grove of red and yellow flowers, and the snake a black mountain underneath him. His weak and defeated coils sliding down into the ocean, Kaliyan cried and praised the great Lord.

nandananda cittacora śri mukunda nin padam
gopabāla vāsudeva meghavarṇa kaitozhām

O Son of Nanda, stealer of our hearts! Auspicious Mukunda, O cowherd boy Vasudeva! the color of dark rain clouds. With folded hands, I pray before Your lotus feet.

ō man mālik (Hindi)

yadā samharate cāyam kūrmōṅgānīva sarvaśaḥ
indriyāṇiyāṇi indriyārthēbhyaḥ tasya prajñā pratiṣṭhitā

One who can withdraw his senses from sense objects, as the tortoise withdraws its limbs into its shell, is established in true wisdom. (Bh. Gita 2.58)

ō man mālik! man kō rōkō
jāl hi jāl bichāēṅ
bēkābū hōkar māyā mēṅ
nāc hi nāc nacāēṅ... ō man mālik

O Lord, please stop this mind ensnared in the net of worldly objects. I lose all control of this illusion and keep dancing to its tune.

jin viṣayōṅ kō bhōg kē chōḍā
lauṭ lauṭ vahī jāēṅ
bharamōṅ kō upajāēṅ har pal

janamō mēṅ bhaṭkāēṅ
jāl hi jāl bichāēṅ
jāl hi jāl bichāēṅ

Again and again my mind returns to the objects that I once enjoyed and abandoned. Cultivating delusions each moment, this mind makes me wander in life after life. It relentlessly casts its net.

ō man mālik! man kō rōkō

O Lord, please stop my mind.

bāndhē man hī gyān kī sīmā
satya samajh nahīṅ āē
kāl dēś is kē hathakaṇḍē kōī pār nā pāēṅ
jitnā bhī iskō bahalāō utnā hī bahakāēṅ
jāl hi jāl bichāēṅ... ō man mālik!

This imprisoned mind does not understand that knowledge and Truth lie beyond its limits. Nobody can overcome the trickery of time and space. No matter how hard I try, this mind relentlessly spreads its net and carries me away.

ōmkāra svaramezhum (Malayalam)

ōmkāra svaramezhum niramāla cārtti
pon sūrya kiraṇattin śōbha tūki
kalitan prabhāvēna vikampita svāntē
dhīra-samīranāy aṇayū ambē

O Mother, adorned with the colorful garland of OM, and radiant with the rays of golden sunlight, the ways of the Kali Yuga agitate my heart (the present age of moral decline). Come to me as a gentle breeze of consolation.

virahattin vēnalil ñān taḷarnnu
hṛdi-śōbhayēkum nī eṅgu pōyi
akalayāy ñānō mizhinūttirunnu
āśakiraṇangaḷ hā poliññu

I am undone by the scorching heat of separation. O light of my heart, where have You gone? I gaze afar in despairing expectation.

ambām yajāmi anaghām namāmi
śyāmām smarāmi bhāmām bhajāmi

O Mother, I surrender my life and bow down to You, O untainted One. Remembering You, O dark One, I sing the praises of Your glory.

nātidūre mṛdu svanam kēṭṭu
citteviḷaṅgunnu ennu connu
sāntvanam ēki kṛpāvarṣam ēki
cērttu tirike sudīpta mārgē

Nearby, I heard a soft voice: "I reside in Your heart." That voice showered my soul with divine grace, a soothing balm, restoring me to the path of illumination.

O Mother, when will I live your dream (English)

O Mother, when will I live your dream for me?
If only I knew how to spread Your love and peace.
When will I see each moment as Your gift?
When will I smile, always feeling Your presence?
When will I serve, pouring myself selflessly?
When will I hear Your sweet words deep within?

When will I care with all my heart for Mother Nature?
When will I tread the path You have led for me?

On the banks of the river (English)

On the banks of the river,
by the sacred Yamuna,
there's a dance by the water
of the gopis and Kṛṣṇa.

Smiles on their faces,
everyone plays and
sings with the flute of gopāla.
Chiming of bracelets,
jingle of anklets
ring to the beat of mṛdanga.

Singing their longing,
dancing their joy.
hari govinda govinda gopāla
hari govinda govinda gopāla

Losing themselves in the
rhythm of love, they
sway hand in hand with gopala.
Under the moonlight,
all through the night, they
pray in the sands of Yamuna.

oru naḷil ñān en (Kannada version)

ontudina nānu kṛṣṇana kāṇuvē
koḷalgāna mādhuri kēḷuvē
sundara adharadi muraḷiya nūduvā
kṛṣṇana darśanā nā paḍēvē

āgenna janma saphalavāguvudū
andu nā ānanda pānamāḍi
unmatta bhaktiya uttuṅga neleyali
nintu ānandadi nartisuvē

ī jīvarāśigaḷigādhāra nīnu
īśa nīnu jagatpālakanu
kālaviḷamba māḍadē bandu
darśanā nīḍi santayisu

oru nōṭṭam-ēkāttat-entē (Malayalam)

oru nōṭṭam-ēkāttat-entē? ammē
onnum uriyāḍāttat-entē
mizhiyōrum nanayunnu karaḷōram pukayunnu
citta-tāpam perukunnu

O Mother, why do you not look at me. Why do you not speak to me? My eyes fill with tears and my heart burns in sorrow.

pizhakaḷ-adhikam bhavikkām – ende
kazhivil aham negaḷikkām

avyāja-kāruṇya-mūrttē – nīyen
aparādham ellām porukkū

I may have done many bad deeds. I may be very proud of my abilities. O Mother, the embodiment of pure compassion, please forgive all my faults.

hṛdayam nuruṅgum vyathakaḷ – ammē
eṅgine uḷḷil-otukkum?
kanivin kaṭākṣam coriññāl – ślatha
hṛdayattil śāntiyēkīḍu

How can I bear this pain cutting through my heart? Bestow your compassionate glance on me and grant peace to my sorrowing heart.

karuṇārdra nētram patiññāl – manam
amṛtābdhi-tannil-ārāḍum
oru mātrayī ūzhī viṭṭu – pon
cirakārnnen manamaṅg-uyarum

When your compassionate glance falls upon me, my heart will bathe in ambrosial bliss. For a moment, my heart will leave its earthly moorings, and soar into the vast sky of Your radiant Self.

oru vitumbal mātram (Malayalam)

oru vitumbal mātram uḷḷil ninn-uyaravē
ariyunnu ñān-inn-aśaktan
oru tuḷḷi nīrkaṇam kaṇkaḷil nirayavē
ariyunnu ñān etra dhanyan

As a sob racks my soul, I realize I am helpless. And as tears fill my eyes, I realize how blessed I am.

anaghē anantatē amalē anāmikē
atiśuddha caritē laḷitē sulaḷitē laḷitē
anaghē anantatē amalē anāmikē

O sinless One, eternal, pure, beyond name and form! You are indescribably charming and graceful. O sinless One, eternal, pure, beyond name and form!

ulapōle eriyunn-oruḷttaṭam
kanivinde uravāl nanacc-uyirēku

Grant new life to my heart, burning in grief like embers in a furnace. Bathe it in the cool waters of Your compassion.

orumātra nīyonnu karutukil
uzhalum-en uyir ninde aṭimalaril-aṇayum

If Your grace falls on me for even an instant, my wandering heart will find its way to Your lotus feet.

jananavum maraṇavum marayiṭṭu-nilkkātta
mahitatama bhūmikayil-amarum

I will merge into the exalted land where birth and death do not exist.

pāhimām paramēśvarī (Malayalam)

pāhimām paramēśvarī paripāhimām hṛdayēśvarī
pāhimām bhaktavatsalē paripāhimām karuṇālayē
vāṇimātē vīṇāpāṇī vilasiḍēṇamen rasanayil
jñānadātē prēmamūrtē vāṇiḍēṇamen mānasē

Protect me, O supreme Goddess! Save me, O goddess of my heart! Protect me, O compassionate one! Save me, O abode of mercy! O Mother of Speech, You hold a vīṇa in your hands. Please dwell on my tongue. O bestower of knowledge and embodiment of love, please dwell in my heart.

mōhanidrayil āṇḍupōyatu koṇḍu cētanayattivaḷ
etrayō aparādha-karmam ceytupōy jagadambikē
duritavāriṇi triguṇakāriṇi saguṇa-nirguṇa-kāriṇī
pāhipāhi bhavāni tāvaka pādapankajam āśrayam

Sunk in the slumber of delusion, I move about without awareness. O Mother of the universe, how many mistakes I have made! O dispeller of sorrows, You are cause of the three attributes (of sattva, rajas and tamas), as well as the substratum of both attributes and the Attribute-less. Save me, O Mother. Your lotus feet are my only refuge.

māyavīśiya mōhavalayil peṭṭu ñānī nāḷvare
mōhajālam aruttumāttuka amba nin karavalliyāl
dīnavatsalē nī grahikkaṇē ende durbala kaittalam
cērkkaṇē tava padamalaril vīṇu kēzhumī ēzhayē

Till now the net of ignorance cast by Your maya has ensnared me. O Mother, please break this spell. O friend of the distressed, please grab hold of my weak hand. I am crying for help. Please draw me, to Your feet.

pannagaśāyi pārthasārathi (Kannada)

pannagaśāyi pārthasārathi
paramavēdaneyā pārugāṇisu
śyāma sundarā śāśvata sukhakara
śaraṇu śaraṇu rādhākṛṣṇā

O Lord Viṣṇu, you repose on Àdiśeṣa, the thousand-headed serpent. O Lord Kṛṣṇa, you were Arjuna's charioteer. Please remove the pain of miseries. O beautiful dark-skinned God, You bestow eternal peace. I take refuge in You, O Rādhākṛṣṇā.

gōpakumārā gōpināthanē
gōvardhana giridhāri
garuḍagamana jaya gānavilōlā
gōvindā hē bālagōpālā

O Lord of the gōpis (milkmaids) and gōpas (cowherd boys), You held aloft Mount Gōvardhana. O lover of divine music, Your vehicle is Garuḍa (eagle). Hail Gōvindā! Hail child Gōpālā!

rādhēkṛṣṇā kṛṣṇā rādhēkṛṣṇā
rāsavilōlā hē rādhēkṛṣṇā

Hail Rādhā-kṛṣṇā, who loves the rāsa dance!

madanamōhanā madhusūdanā
muraḷī manōharā mādhava
bhaktavatsalā bhavabhaya haranē
bēḍuvē anukṣaṇa bhāsuranē

O mesmerizing one, Mādhava (Lord of Lakṣmi), Madhusūdanā (slayer of the demon Madhu), the sound of Your flute is enchanting. You compassionately redeem Your devotees from transmigration and fear. O Radiant One, I pray to You incessantly!

pittā endrazhaittālum (Tamil)

pittā endrazhaittālum varuvāyē
perum cittā endrazhaittālum varuvāyē
vittāgi maramāgi viḷangum pemmānē

cittattai śivamākki taruvāyē

O Lord, whether we call You "mad" or "supreme consciousness," You always come to us. O Lord, You are the seed as well as the tree. Please make my mind one with the Absolute.

sottāle pittāga tirivārē – silar
cittrinpa pittāga alaivārē
pattāḷin adhikāram peṭrālē silapērō
pittēri talaikīzhāy naḍappārē

Some are mad after wealth, some are mad after sense pleasures. Some are head over heels after power and position.

ettālē teḷivāgum empittam – emmai
sattāna śivamāga yām uṇarvōm
muttāna arivālē pittellām teḷivāgum
attāvē ataivēṇḍi paṇindōmē

When will our mad minds get clarity? We shall awaken when You reveal the pure Absolute in us. Pure knowledge will dispel our madness. O Lord, we bow down to You and beg for that knowledge.

mādorubhāgan ānavā
malaimagaḷ manadai koṇḍavā
mālayan pōttrum nāyagā
sadguru nāthā dēśikā
śivaśiva harahara purahara madahara
bhayahara bhavahara śankarā

O Lord, You stole the heart of Parvati and You share one half of Her (Ardhanareeshwara - the Lord who is half Shiva and half Shakti). You are my Satguru, Lord Shiva, worshipped by all. You destroy our fears and our ego. You help us cross this ocean of samsara. We bow down to You.

prabhuji tērā darśan (Hindi)

prabhuji tērā darśan kaisē pāvuṅ
mānava janma nā vyarth gavāvūṅ

Dear Lord, how do I obtain Your Darshan (holy glimpse). Let me not squander this human birth.

tan tō hai ye, mal kī ghaṭarī, māyā man bharmāyē
dēh hī mēṅ hun, aisā samajkar, man ko yē bhaṭkāyē
apnā man hī mailā hai tō, ungalī kiskō dikhāūṅ
apnī hālat par ṣarmāūṅ

This body is a collection of dirt and negativities. And Maya (the illusory world) distracts the mind. It makes us identify with the body and deludes us. When my own mind is dirty, at whom shall I point a finger. I feel ashamed at my plight.

vintī hai, hē bhagavan
ab dē dō tum darśan

Dear Lord, please hear my humble request and give me Your darshan.

har ik prāṇī, har ik kaṇ mēṅ, tum hī hō prabhu rahatē
īśāvāsyam idam sarvam, aisā ved hai kahatē
bāhar bhī aur andar bhī tujhē, kyōṅ mēṅ dēkh nā pāūṅ
kahāṅ sē mēṅ vō āṅkhē lāūṅ

It is You who exist in every life, in each and every atom. The Vedas say the entire universe is pervaded by the Supreme. Why can I not see You outside and inside? O Lord, where shall I obtain such eyes?

prēm sē gāō (Hindi)

prēm sē gāō prēm sē nācō
prēm kī dēvī kī jay jay bōlō

Sing with love, dance with love, chant the glories of the Goddess of love.

prēm kē sāgar sē jō bhī hai jāyē
māyā jāl mēṅ vō phaṅsa jāyē
prēm kē sāgar mēṅ jō ḍūb jāyē
amṛt pīyē vō amar ban jāyē

The net of Illusion will trap the one who swims away from the ocean of Love. One who drowns in the ocean of love will drink Amritam and become Immortal.

prēm sē bōlō prēm sē dēkhō
prēm kī dēvī kī jay jay bōlō

Speak with Love, look with Love, chant the glories of the Goddess of Love.

jismēṅ ahaṅkār aur ho mamkār
aisē bandē kī hō jāyē hār
tyāg kē sab kuch jō bhī āyē
ōṁkār mēṅ vō sadā bas jāyē

One who is arrogant and attached will be defeated. One who gives up everything will reach the state of Omkar.

prēm sē japō prēm sē bhajō
prēm kī dēvī kī jay jay bōlō

Chant mantra with Love. Sing bhajan with Love. Chant the glories of the Goddess of Love.

prēm sē gāō (prēm sē nācō)
prēm sē bōlō (prēm sē dēkhō)
prēm sē japō (prēm sē bhajō)
prēm mēṅ līn hō, prēm ban jāō

Chant mantra with Love. Sing bhajans with Love. Chant the glories of the Goddess of Love.

prēm kī dēvī kī jay jay bōlō

Chant the glories of the Goddess of Love.

prēma-gaṅgē ammē (Malayalam)

prēma-gaṅgē ammē amṛta-gaṅgē
jñāna-gaṅgē ammē prāṇa-gaṅgē

O Mother, You are the Ganga of love, the Ganga of immortality, the Ganga of knowledge and the Ganga that flows as our life force.

kavitayāy uḷḷilēkk-ozhuki-ettunnu nī
prēma-gaṅgē ammē amṛtēśvari
en-manō-mālinyam kazhuki ozhukkuvān
enn-uḷḷil vannu nī gaṅgayāy

You flow into my heart as poetry, O Mother, eternal goddess, Ganga of love. You have come as a Ganga within me, to wash away all the impurities of my mind!

mizhi-pūṭṭi nin snēha tīre-irikkumbōḷ
uḷḷil-ozhukunnu śānti-gaṅga

ā prēma-gaṅgayil ozhukiṭaṭṭe ammē
karma-bhāṇḍhaṅgaḷ ozhukkiṭaṭṭe

Sitting with eyes closed on the banks of Your love, a Ganga of peace flows within. O Mother, may the bundle of my karma float away in the river of Your love

sarvatum ēttu-vāṅgunna nin salilamō
ā prēma-hṛdaya-pravāham-allē
ā prēma-gaṅgayil muṅgi nīrāṭi ñān
mukti-āyīṭaṭṭe nityam-ammē

The love flowing from Your heart accepts everything. May I dive deep into Your Ganga of love, and become ever free, O Mother.

puṭṭa puṭṭa kṛṣṇā (Kannada)

puṭṭa puṭṭa kṛṣṇā... muddu nalumē kṛṣṇā
ōḍi ōḍi bārō kamala kṛṣṇā
nīlamēghavarṇā... ghanaśyāma kṛṣṇa
mōhana kṛṣṇā... madhura kṛṣṇā...

O little Krishna, darling one, come running to Mother, O beautiful one. Your complexion is like dark rain clouds. Sweet Krishna, You are truly enchanting!

pītāmbara vastra uḍisēlamma yiruvalū
navilugarī karadi piṭidu kādiruvaḷu
vastravuṭṭu gariya dharise ōḍi bā kṛṣṇā
hāḍuhāḍi nalidāḍalu bēga bā kṛṣṇa...

Mother is here to dress You with yellow robes. She waits for You with a peacock feather in her hand. O Krishna, wearing the yellow robes and adorned with the peacock feather, come running to Mother.

hālubeṇṇe siddhagoḷisi kāturadi kādihaḷu
koḷala daniya saviyalendu amma ninna nenesihaḷu
hālu kuṭidu beṇṇe savidu koḷala nūtu kṛṣṇā...
hāḍuhāḍi kunidāṭalu bēga bā kṛṣṇā...

Mother waits for You eagerly with milk and butter. She thinks of You constantly, and enjoys the enchanting the melody of Your flute. O Krishna, drink the milk, eat the butter, and play the flute. Come quickly to sing and dance with Mother.

jōjō lālī... lālī kṛṣṇā...
ammana maṭilalī malagu kṛṣṇā...

O Krishna, let Mother sing a lullaby to You. Come and rest in Mother's lap.

rām hamārē śyām hamārē (Hindi)

rām hamārē śyām hamārē
param pitā vō sirjan hārē

Our Ram, our Shyam is the Supreme Father, the Creator of us all!

sab lōkōṅ kē pālanhārē
jan-jan kē vō hi rakhvārē
antaryāmi, sab jag-svāmi
sab sē nyārē dil kē pyārē

He sustains all the worlds and protects one and all! He is the Lord immanent in the whole universe, most unique and dear to everyone's heart!

yōg mē vō hi bhōg mē vō hi
jap mē vō hi tap mē vō hi
milan mēṇ vō bicchaḍan mēṇ vō hi

tan aur man hōtē ujiyārē

In union, he alone is and in enjoyment too. He alone is the substratum of japa and austerity! In association as well as in solitude, He alone is! Knowing this illumines body and mind!

sṛṣṭi kē kaṇ-kaṇ ādhārē
sab bhēdōṅ kē bhēdan hārē
brahmāṇḍōṅ mēṅ camak rahē vō
ban kar anagin sūraj tārē

He is the substratum of every particle of creation, the Truth that penetrates all mysteries! He shines brilliantly throughout the Universe in the form of countless suns and galaxies!

rām rām rām sīyā rām rām rām
śyām śyām śyām rādhē śyām śyām śyām

rām hī rām (Hindi)

rām hī rām sab kuch rām
bhaj lē bandē rām kā nām

O man, everything is nothing but Ram, so chant Ram's name!

janm bhī rām maraṇ bhī rām
dharm bhī rām karm bhī rām
it bhī rām ut bhī rām
tujh mēṅ rām mujh mēṅ rām

In birth is Ram, and in death too is Ram; faith is Ram, action is Ram. Here is Ram, there is Ram! Ram is in you, and in me too!

mān bhī rām prēm bhī rām
dhyān bhī rām gyān bhī rām
śravaṇ bhī rām manan bhī rām
sparś bhī rām daras bhī rām

Compassion is Ram. Love is Ram. Meditation is Ram, and knowledge too is Ram! Sravana (listening) is Ram, and manana (contemplation) is Ram. Touch is Ram, and vision too is Ram!

andar rām bāhar rām
sūkṣm bhī rām sthūl bhī rām
yukti bhī rām mukti bhī rām
śakti bhī rām bhakti bhī rām

Within is Ram, and outside is Ram. The subtle is Ram, and so is the gross. The means is Ram and liberation too is Ram. Strength is Ram, and devotion is Ram!

jay jay rām jay jay rām
jay jay rām jay jay rām
jay jay rām rām rāma
jay jay rām rām rāma
jay jay rām rām rāma

Victory to Lord Ram!

raṅg jā tu maiyyā (Punjabi)

raṅg jā tu maiyyā dē raṅg vicc
raṅg raṅg kē raṅg raṅg jāṇā hai

Color yourself in the colors of the Divine Mother. Color yourself until you are immersed in Her.

kudrat nū vēkhā ō maiyyā - tērē
rūp dā cōlā pāyā hai - dil
diyāṅ gehrāyiyāṅ vicc
ehsās dā bīj lagāyā hai
niman hai tērā ō maiyyā - is
sāh vicc sāh pāyā hai
jis muktī nū
jis muktī nū lab lab thakēyā - tērē
caraṇā vicc pāyā hai

The beautiful nature around reflects Your enchanting form. Deep in our heart, You have sown the seed of Your wondrous presence. I bow to You, O Mother. In my unceasing longing for You, my every breath has merged with Your breath. The liberation I searched for, I found at Your feet.

adbhut eh nagmā ō maiyyā - prēm
tērē nē racāyā hai
śabdāṅ dē kērē tō bāhar
maunam nē sajāyā hai
śukar hai tērā ō maiyyā
is sat nū darśāyā hai
is jīvan dā
is jīvan dā sār tu hī
bākī sab ik māyā hai

Your love has created this wonderful composition, O Mother. It originated in silence and is beyond words. I thank You Mother, for revealing the Truth that the essence of this life is You. All the rest is illusion.

raṅg jā raṅg jā raṅg jā raṅg jā

maiyyādē raṅg vicc

Color yourself in the colors of the Divine Mother!

ravikula-tilaka (Sanskrit)

ravikula-tilaka
avikala-phalada
vara-guṇa-nilaya
khara-mada-haraṇa

O jewel of Ravikula (the mighty kings of the Solar Dynasty), readily you bestow flawless boons. Abode of supreme qualities. Destroyer of ego (the demon Khara).

rāma śrī rāma – ō rāma
rāma śrī rāma
O auspicious Lord Rama!
atulita-vaibhava
vidhi-bhava-sannuta
madana-manōhara
sadaya-kṛpākara

Your glory is matchless. Brahma, the creator, and Lord Shiva worship You. You are the handsome Lord who enchants all, ever bestowing merciful compassion.

vibhō rāmacandra
prabhō mānavēndra
rāma.. rāma... rāma...
cidānanda-sindhō
sadārāddhya-bandhō

O Lord Rama, you are the all-pervasive Absolute, supreme among men. Your nature is pure consciousness and bliss. You are our heart's closest friend, ever worthy of worship.

param dhāma-rāma
varam dēhi rāma
śūra vīra śyāma
prēma-rūpa-rāma

O Rama, ultimate abode, kindly grant us liberation. Dark-hued, courageous and valorous, You are the embodiment of pure love!

Reflect on life (English)

Reflect on life, life is a story.
The writer is here in all Her glory.
Read every page, a moral shines through,
life's greatest fortune is being with You.

You're always here, living with me,
in silence, dreams, distant memory,
feelings of love, shining bright light,
nature and peace deep inside.

Deep in the page, life is sacred.
You are creation, You weave the web.
Remember truth, life comes alive.
You are the power through time.

jagadīśvarī sarvēśvarī
praṇēśvarī mahādēvī

Goddess of the Universe, Goddess of all things, Goddess of life force, the great Goddess.

ruṭhā hai kyōṅ mērē lāl (Hindi)

ruṭhā hai kyōṅ mērē lāl
ab tō haṅs dē zarā
maiyā kahē sun rē śyām
braj kā tuhē dulārā
itnā bhōlā-bhālā
itnā bhōlā-bhālā

Why are you upset my darling, won't you smile just a little? Mother calls you, O Shyam, darling of Vrindavan. Krishna is so sweet and innocent.

ākē galē lag jā rē kānhā
chōḍ de yē gussā
kyā maiyā kē hāthōṅ se
mākhan nahīṅ khānā
ab tō mān lē śyām
ab tō haṅs le zarā

Come and hug me, O Krishna, leaving aside your anger. Won't you accept some butter from your mother? At least now, O Shyam, please relent and smile a little.

naṭkhaṭ hai merā kānhā nahīṅ
dahī mākhan curāyā nahīṅ
jhūṭh kahē sab gvālīn nē... hā
itnā bhōlā-bhālā

My Krishna is not naughty. Surely he did not steal butter. The cowherd girls lie. You are so sweet and innocent.

tū hai merā nandalālā
mēri āṅkhōṅ kā tārā
itnā tū sundar itnā tū pyārā
sab kē man kō harnē vālā
itnā bhōlā-bhālā

You are my darling son, the brilliant star of my eyes, so beautiful, so darling. You win over everyone, so sweet, so innocent.

sācō tērō nām (Hindi)

sācō tērō nām rāmā
jhūṭhē jag kē kām

O Rama, the only real Truth is your name. All else in the world is false.

kyōṅ kartā hē mērā mērā
yūṅ kartā is bhram kō ghanērā
kōyī nahīṅ hai jag mē tērā
ant samay tū jāyē akēlā

Why do you increase your confusion by repeating over and over 'I' and 'mine'. In this world, there is no one for you to call your own. In the end you will have to leave this world alone.

kyā lāyā thā sāth jagat mēṅ
kyā lēkar ab jāyēgā
muṭṭhī bāndhē āyā thā tū
hāth pasārē jāyēgā

When you come to this world, do you bring anything with you? And when you leave, can you take anything along? You were born with your little fists clenched, and you will leave with empty hands.

kyōṅ nahīṅ ātā rām śaraṇ mēṅ
kyōṅ yūṅ jīvan vyarth karē
sauṅp unhē hī jīvan ḍor
rām nām bas mukh sē bōl

Why not take refuge in Lord Rama? Why waste your life in vain like this? Offer your life to Him, and forever chant his divine name.

tērō nām... sācō nām... tērō nām... ik tērō nām...
jay rām sīyā rām jay rām sīyā rām
jay rām jay jay rām

O Rama, Your name is the only Truth! Victory to Ram and Sita!

sadāśivā mahēśvarā (Malayalam)

sadāśivā mahēśvarā bhaktalōka rakṣakā
tribhuvanēśvarā jagad-nivāsa śrīgirīśvarā

O auspicious Shiva, great God, the protector of Your devotees. The Lord of the three worlds, O Jagannivasa. Your abode is the mountain Kailasa.

arivin ponprabha coriññu antaraṅgam-āke
nin prēma-kīrttanaṅgaḷ pāṭi ujjvalippū mānasam
nin kṛpā-kaṭākṣam-ēttu pūvaṇiññu nilkkuvān
uḷḷil āyiram tarukkaḷ tiṅgi viṅgiṭunnitā
bhava hara hara śaṅkarā pura hara hara śaṅkarā

My inner self is effulgent in the golden light of Your knowledge. My heart is ablaze singing love-songs to You. A thousand young trees jostle in my mind, awaiting your loving glance to bloom and flower.

sāndra-rāgatāḷam-ārnnu pāḍi nṛttam-āṭuvān

hṛdaya-tamburu uṇarnnu śruti pakarnnu
mōdamāy
praṇava-mantram kātil ōti pulkiṭunnu mānasam
ēttupāṭi kāvyanadikaḷ ozhukiṭunnu puṇyamāy
bhava hara hara śaṅkarā pura hara hara śaṅkarā

The tamburu of my heart waits joyfully to play the music of your eternal song. My heart embraces the pranava mantra resounding in my ears. Many rivers of song flow as punya (merit) from my soul.

bhakti-gāna-sudhayil onnu cērnn-amarnn-
aliyuvān
arivil-ēri arivu mātramāyi onnu cēruvān
amṛtam-ākkū puṇya-janmam saphalamāy
dhanyamāy
nityataye pulkuvān jīvan-mukti tēḍuvān
bhava hara hara śaṅkarā pura hara hara śaṅkarā

I want to merge in ambrosial songs of devotion to You. I want to realize true knowledge and become one with it. Let this human birth be fulfilled and blessed. May I embrace eternity and attain liberation.

sādi tōjāle (Tulu)

sādi tōjāle satyōda sādi tōjāle
nemmadida sukha badukugu sādi tōjāle
ātmaśakti korulemma kaṣṭolen sahisare
paramapāvane dēvi īrē namaku āsare

Show me the way to the Truth, show me the way to a peaceful happy life. O Mother give me the Self-confidence to bear sorrows. O sacred pure Devi, You are my only refuge.

nanala bōḍu nanala bōḍu namak panpi āselu
dūramaltuṇḍu manaḥśānti samādhāno
svārttha buddhi uppunaga pōparīr dūranē
divya jñāna bhakti kordu kāpulemma bēkane
mahammāyē paramēśvari dēvi ambikē

So many hidden desires torment us, snatching our peace of mind. Our selfish mind ever takes us far away. Give us divine knowledge and devotion, O Mother. O supreme Goddess of the great illusion, O my eternal Mother, save us.

jīvanada duḥkhōlegu manassonje kāraṇa
satsaṅga kīrttaneḍe untālemma manassunu
ātma yān śarīro attu panpi bōdha korpadu
dāḍalemma bhava sāgara karuṇāmayi dēvi
mahammāyē paramēśvari dēvi ambikē

The fickle mind is the sole cause of life's sorrows. Bless us through satsang and kirtan to purify our minds so we can uplift ourselves through right knowledge. Help us cross this ocean of transmigration (cycle of birth and death), O supreme and compassionate Goddess of the great illusion, O my eternal Mother.

śakti tū sab jīv (Hindi)

śakti tū sab jīv cētani
śānti tū para brahm rūpiṇi
vāṇī tū catur vēda rūpiṇi
mā catur daś lōk rūpiṇi

O Primal Energy, You are the consciousness in every living being. You are true Peace. O Goddess of Speech in the form of the Vedas, O Mother, You are the world.

mā tum hī sarv svarūpiṇi
mā tum hī brahm svarūpiṇi
mā tum hī bhaktārttī nāśini
mā tum hī mukti pradāyini

O Mother You are All. You are the ultimate, the One who destroys the suffering of devotees. Indeed You are the giver of freedom.

vaiṣṇavī sab mē virājati hai
śankarī śiv kē priyēśvarī tū
śāradā sab kō jñān pradāyini
rādhikā hari kē rās rasēśvarī

As Vaishnavi, you reside in All. As Shankari you are the beloved of Shiva. As Saraswati you bestow knowledge and as Radha you are the beloved of Krishna.

rañjitē sabkī tum hī jananī
nanditē dil mēṅ sadā rahtī
ham karē bintī sadā tujhsē
bhakti dē hamkō kṛpā kar kē

O Mother, You are the One that delights us and lives in our hearts. We implore You to bless us with devotion.

ambē... jagadambē... jagadambē...
jagadambē mā... jagadambē mā...

O Mother... O Mother of the Universe...

samasta līḷārē (Odiya)

samasta līḷārē pūri rahi acha āhā

māyāra hi rūpa tūmo svarupa hi māyā
prabhāmayī mā gō tūmē mōhari jībanē
usā hōi vikiraṇa kiridia prabhā

You are present in all your leelas. You are the form of maya. O radiant Mother, please come to my life and light up everything like the morning sun.

sannidhi tūmara jēbē ēhi prāṇa pāē
apūrba prēma srōtarē abagāhi jāē
tūmari dibya tējarē nitya līna hōī
bhaba-duḥkha rāji mōra jāu āji bohi

When my soul senses your presence, I get immersed in a stream of pure love, absorbed in divine radiance. Wash away the miseries of this worldly existence .

mā gō... mā gō... mā gō... mā gō...

O Mother...

tūmaku khōji pāibi mō ādhāra bindu
ē pathika bāṭabaṇā kāhi kētē dinuṅ
paramānandara bara pāu mōra ātmā
jībana sārthaka mōra kari diā ammā

O my very source of existence, how long will I wander in search of You? O Mother, granting the boon of supreme bliss, please make my life blessed.

taba darasana mō ēkāī āsā bhabē
ākuḷē ḍākuchi mā diya dēkhā ēbē

Your vision is my only desire in life. O Mother, I pray fervently, please appear before me!

śēr tē savār āyī (Punjabi)

śēr tē savār āyī
ban kē bahār āyī
baldē saṇ sār vic
ṭandhī phuhār āyī

Like the spring, She has come riding the lion. In this burning world, She comes like a cool breeze.

jay mātā dī jay mātā dī
jay mātā dī jay mātā dī
jay mātā dī jay mātā dī

Victory to Mother Goddess!

vēkhō lōkō ajab najārā
mādā darbār pyārā
mōkā nā gavāvō lōkō
caraṇā dā lēlō sahārāb
gyān hōr pagtī dā
ban kē avatār āyī
ditā satsaṅg sānu
sēvā dī rāh dikhāyī

People! (hey everyone!), see this wonderful sight of Mother's loving darbaar (the palace where Mother sits). Don't miss this chance people. Take help of Mother's Lotus Feet by taking refuge in them. Mother has come as an incarnation of knowledge as well as devotion. Mother gives us Her words of wisdom and shows us a way to serve the world. Jai Mata Di (Jai to Mother Goddess)

sārē jag tō lōkī āndē

mādā āśīś pāṇ dē
mādiyā pēndā gāṇ dē
raj kē khuśī manōṇ dē
pagtā nu ṭarśan dēndī
unāntē dē duḥkh har-lēntī
gur dā rūp tāran karkē
pav sāgar pār lagāndī

People come from all over the world to receive Mother's blessings. They sing bhajans and rejoice in Her presence. Mother gives darshan to all devotees and removes their sorrows. In the form of Guru, She takes her devotees across the ocean of samsara.

śibjē bhōlā (Bengali)

śibjē bhōlā monjē khōlā śibērmōtō nāc dēkhi
śōṣān ghāṭē ghūrē bērāy, cāy mēkhē ēy pāgōlṭi
śibjē nācē apōn tālē, śibēr mōtō mōnpābi
joyrē bhōlā bom bom bhōlā joy bhōlēnāth śambhōji

Shiva is simple with an open mind. Have you seen a dance like Shiva's? He runs around in the crematorium with ash on his body. Shiva dances to his own rhythm, but will you get a mind like Shiva's? Victory to the innocent Shiva.

pārbōtitāy rūp bhulē bhāy, śibēr kāccē jāyēbuji
pāglā bhōlā apon bhōlā āmiyōtārē tāykhuji
śib śibānir roṅ dēkhē nāc-nācē-nāc nikhil bhōr
śēy tālētē tāldiyēci nāci āmi rātri bhōr
joyrē bhōlā bom bom bhōlā joy bhōlēnāth śambhōji

Goddess Parvati forgets her beauty and runs after Shiva. The crazy Shiva, innocent Shiva! I also am trying to find Him. Seeing the dance of Shiva and Shivani, all join in the Divine Dance. Catching his rhythm, I too dance night and day. Victory to the innocent One. Victory to Shiva!

jōṭādhāri śibjē cārā ārjē kīccu nāy rē mōr
ḍulē ḍulē biśvaghōrē mōn pāglā bhōbhēr ghōr
mōn bōbāni pāglē śāmi pār kōrāv mā bhābēr ḍōr
mā jē bhōlē hātjē tulē nāc-nāc-nāc nācrē jōr
joyrē bhōlā bom bom bhōlā joy bhōlēnāth śambhōji

Without Shiva, my Lord with dread-locked hair (beyond worldliness), I am nothing. Shiva's divine dance intoxicates my mind. My mind is Bhavani and my beloved is this mad ascetic, Shiva. Now take me out of this mad world of illusion. Taking Mother's Name, lift your hands in prayer. Dance, dance, dance in ecstasy. Victory to the innocent One. Victory to Shiva!

joy rē bhōlā śambhōji – bom bom bhōlā śambhōji

Victory to the innocent One! Victory to Shiva!

siṭrinbam nāḍum (Tamil)

siṭrinbam nāḍum sirumatiyinai
sīrākki sīrārum pērariviṇai
aḷḷittarum annaiyē arpudamē
porpadamē em narpadamē

O mother, you generously give us the Supreme knowledge to tame our ignorant mind which keeps seeking worldly pleasures. Your Feet are our sole refuge

vazhikāṭṭa nīyum marandu-viṭṭāl
vazhimāri ēngō pōy viḍuvōm

tagudi illāmal irundālum
un tāḷgaḷ nāḍi vandōmē

If you forget to show us the way, we will be lost somewhere. Even if we are undeserving, we come in search of your Lotus Feet

gativēṇḍi ēngum unsēygaḷ
vidhitūṇḍum vazhiyil sellāmal
madi mayakkam tannai teḷivākki
ativēgam undan tāḷsērppāy

Your children long for refuge. Please make sure we don't go on the wrong path. Please bestow clarity on our clouded minds and let us quickly surrender at your Lotus Feet

azhiyāda ānandam taruvāḷ
annayiḍam tañcam aḍaindiḍuvōm
nilayillā ulagil irundālum
nilayāna tuṇaiyāy irundiḍuvāḷ

Let us take refuge in our Mother. She will give us everlasting bliss. She will be our permanent protector in this impermanent world.

śiva śiva śiva śiva uraittiḍuvāyē (Tamil)

śiva śiva śiva śiva uraittiḍuvāyē
bhava-bhayam tīrndiḍa śivamayam angē
śiva śiva śivāya bhava bhaya harāya

Chanting "Shiva-Shiva" destroys the fear of the cycle of birth and death and then Godliness pervades. Salutations to Lord Shiva, destroyer of the fear of the cycle of birth and death.

aruḷ aruḷ aruḷ ena aruḷpasi koṇḍāl
uṇarndiru uṇavadē pusi adai enbān
kaṭinam ayyā uṇarndiruppadu endrāl
undudal nān uṇḍu sulabham adenbān

To the desperate ones, hungry for Grace, He says, "Be aware. Awareness is the food. Partake of it." If you say you are unable to get awareness, He says, "I am there with you to inspire you; so, you will easily get it."

ulaimanam ulagiyal viṣayattil tōyndāl
nijamalla udariḍu tuccham adenbān
kaṭinam ayyā manam velvadu endrāl
tuṇai ena nān uṇḍu bhayam edarkkenbān

When the wandering mind gets lost in worldly pursuits, He says, "Worldliness is worthless so cast it aside." If you say that overcoming the mind is difficult, He says, "Why fear when I am there to support you?"

śivōham śivōham (Hindi)

śivōham śivōham
śivōham śivōham
pūrṇ hī bhītar pūrṇ hī bāhar
pūrṇ hī chārōṅ ōr
bhēd nahīṅ bhītar bāhar kā
sarvānand cahuṅ ōr

I am Shiva. I am complete inside, complete outside, complete in every direction. There is no difference between inside and outside. On every side is bliss.

khālī nahīṅ yē śūnya hai pūraṇ
kartā na kōyī kāraṇ
ēk hī tattv sarvatr samāyā
uskī kōkh sē āyā – jag
uskī kōkh sē āyā

This void is actually whole, not empty. There is neither doer nor cause. Only one principle pervades everywhere. And from its womb has emerged this Universe.

nāṭak uskā mañc bhī vō
har bhūmikā bhī hai vō
kāhē na samjhēṅ na jīv hai ham?
saccidānand rūp hai ham
saccidānand rūp hai ham

The play is of the Supreme. The stage is His too. He plays every role. Why don't we understand that we are not this individual. We are the form of Sat-Chit-Ananda (Existence-Consciousness-Bliss).

sumadhura sundara (Sanskrit)

sumadhura sundara muraḷi vinōdana
kaḷayamunātaṭa cāri harē
naṭavara nūpura-dharaṇa manōhara
vrajayuvatī-manahāri hare

O Lord, You play a sweet and melodious flute while roaming the banks of the Yamuna River. O Lord, You captivate the hearts of the young maidens of Vraja with your beautiful dance and jingling anklets.

hasita-mukhāmbuja natajana-pālana
śritajana-pālana-śīla harē
maṇimaya nūpura-kankaṇa dhāraṇa
manalaya-kāraṇa dēva hare

O Lord, Your smiling face is like a lotus. You protect the righteous and those who take refuge in You. O Lord, You wear jewel-studded anklets and bracelets and You dissolve the mind too.

bāla harē gōpāla harē – jaya
mādhava dīna-dayāla hare

O divine child, O cowherd boy, O Lord of Goddess Lakshmi and protector of the fallen!

śaśimukha śrīdhara mangaḷa-lōcana
hāra-mukuṭadhara dhīra harē
śrīramaṇī-mukha-pankaja bhāskara
śrīrādhāpriya sādhupatē

O Wise One, You have a moon-like face and auspicious eyes. Sporting a garland and crown, You hold Goddess Lakshmi in Your heart. Her face blooms like a lotus on seeing Her effulgent Lord. Radha adores You, O protector of the righteous.

yadukula-nāyaka yavanaharā jaya
yatikula-pūjita śrīla harē
atimṛdu-bhāṣaṇa cirasukha-dāyaka
vrajajanamōhana pāhi hare

O chieftain of the Yadu clan, You slayed Kalayavana (a demon). O Auspicious One, the lineage of saints worships You. You speak softly and bestow eternal well-being on all. O Lord, who enchanted the people of Vraja, please save me!

sun mēri mayyā (Hindi)

sun mēri mayyā māt bhavāni
jag janani mahārāṇi
vinati sunō kalyāṇi

Listen, O my Mother Bhavani, Mother of the Universe, O Empress! Listen to my prayer.

bīt gayē aisē janm yē kitnē
rahā tēri khōj mēṅ sadā
aur na rakhnā dūr mā mujhkō
ab tō galē sē lagālō... mā
mamtā mēṅ nehlā dō

How many lifetimes have passed like this? Always, I remain in search of You. Do not keep me away any longer, O Mother. Hold me close to You at least now. Bathe me in Your love!

kehlānē kō tērī santān
guṇ mā kōyi mujh mē nahīṅ
bālak cāhē hō jaisā bhi
mā mē hai karuṇā hī
karti hai vō kṣamā hī

I am not worthy. I have no excellent quality to be called Your child. However the child may be, the Mother has only compassion, and will always forgive.

ājāvō, mātē darśan dō...

Come, O Mother, give me Your darshan!

tabōnām (Bengali)

tabōnām gānē bhōrē thāk prāṇē
aśiṣō kuśumō śatōdōl
tabōnām dhēnē cūvē jāk mōnē
prēmērō porōśō karōtal

May Your name fill my life. Just as the blessed lotus blooms, may Your name touch my prayers and awaken the bloom of Love.

ēśōhē mohārāj ēśō ēśō nāth
śāth dāu tumi ōgō dhārō mōr hāth
tōmārō śaṅgē raśōtaraṅgē
bādhā hōk hṛd-kamal
bādhā hōk hṛd-kamal

Come, O king of kings. Come, come O Master! Be with me, hold my hand. As I play the divine ras with You, may my heart remain intertwined with Yours.

kikhēlā khēlēcō hori hai mōr
dāuni tō kōnō poricōy
āmār jibōnē tomārō praśārō
śēyi ṭuku śañcōy

O playful Hari, what a play You played without even letting me know. In my life whatever You have bestowed on me, that alone is my treasure.

ebār bēlā hōlō śārā hōlō khēlā
pāṭ gōṭānōr eśēcē jē pālā
tōmārō nāmkhāni amṛtōbāṇi
śēy hōk mōr śombhōl
śēy hōk mōr śombhōl

Now that the play is over, it is time to pack up. Your sweet name is immortal. May that be my only support.

tallī vallī kalpavallī (Telugu)

tallī vallī kalpavallī

O Mother, You are the magical, wish-fulfilling tree!

nēnu puṭṭitinō ōyamma nīke telusu
nā talli nanu kaninā nākēmi telusu
jīvuḍu nēnamma karma-bandhamulu mānpu
śivarūpi nīvamma bādhalanu mānpu

Was I born? Did my mother give me life? I am merely a jīva (individual soul). You are the very essence of Lord Śiva. Please dissolve all my karmic bonds and remove the obstacles in my spiritual path.

nā prāṇa sañcayamu chinnā bhinnamu – nē
paḍē vēdanalu parvata tulyamu
nā vyathalu durvidhulu vivarimpa taramā – dayā-
nidhivammā nī centa cērcukō

My prāṇa (vital breath) is irregular. My problems are huge as a mountain. Sorrow is my lot. How can I explain my problems? You are the repository of compassion. Please draw me close to You.

tappulē yeñcani vātsalya-mūrtivi
giriputri prāṇadā yōgadā sarvadā
kailāsa nilayē pārvati ambā
vaikuṇṭha vāsini ō lakṣmi ambā

O embodiment of compassion, You don't see my faults. You are daughter of the mountain (Pārvati). You bestow everything, including yōga (oneness with God) and prāṇa (vital breath). As Goddess Pārvati You reside in Mount Kailās, the abode of Lord Śiva. In Vaikuṇṭha, the abode of Lord Viṣṇu, You reside as Goddess Lakṣmi.

tañjamena vandōm (Tamil)

tañjamena vandōm dayaipuri vēlā
vañjamilā neñjamadil mañjam koḷḷa vārāy

O most compassionate Lord Muruga, we take refuge in You. Please dwell in this pure heart.

arivirkk-aṇisēr aranār maganē
piravi-piṇitīr piraiyōn maganē
turavigaḷ paṇiyum maraiyin poruḷē
iruvinai nīkkum saravaṇa-bhavanē

O son of Lord Shiva, enhance my wisdom and heal my disease of worldliness. O essence of the Vedas, Saints extol You. O Sharavana (another name for Muruga), take away both sin and merit from me.

anpin vaḍivē arivin suḍarē
iruḷadu nīngi oḷiyum peruga

O embodiment of Love, let the lamp of wisdom dispel the darkness of my ignorance.

aḍiyārkk-aruḷ sēr jñāna-kumarā
eḷiyār maruḷtīr śakti-kumarā
oruvāy mozhiyilai unpēr anḍri
varuvāy vēṇḍiḍa manadil onḍri

O embodiment of wisdom and strength, shower Your grace on this poor child and dispel his fear. My only prayer is that only Your name comes to mind.

inbam tunbam immai marumai
irumai akanḍru orumai uṇara

Help me transcend joy and sorrow, birth and death, and awaken in me the sense of non-duality.

vēlvēl murugā veṭrivēl murugā
śaktivēl murugā jñānavēl murugā

Victory to the wielder of the spear, the powerful and wise one!

teccippū piccippū (Malayalam)

teccippū piccippū onnonnu cērttu ñān
prēmattil kōrttoru mālayuṇḍu
cembakaccēluḷḷa koṇḍayil cērkkānāy
kōla mayilppīli vērēyuṇḍu

I strung a garland of techipu flowers (chrysanthus, a small red flower) and jasmin on a thread of love. I brought a peacock feather that resembles a champa flower to decorate your hair tuft.

ōṭattaṇḍ-onnilāy kinnari-toṅgalum
mañña pizhiññuḷḷa paṭṭum-uṇḍu
ōṭi vāyōṭi vā ōmana-kkaṇṇā nin-
pūmēni kāṇuvān vembalāyi
pūmēni kāṇuvān vembalāyi

I decorated a bamboo flute with a beautiful tassel, and here is a yellow silk cloth. O darling Kanna, come running, come! I long to see your beautiful form.

pālilāy kalkkaṇḍam-iṭṭuḷḷa pāyasam
pāzhāyi-ppōkum nī vannillenkil
nannāy-kaṭaññu ñān cērtta naruveṇṇa
uṇṇuvān-uṇṇi nī vanniṭēṇam

If you do not come, the sweet milk payasam will go waste. O little one, you should come to eat the fresh butter I have churned.

kūṭṭattil-uḷḷa nin caṅgātimārkk-ellām
kūṭe-kkazhikkān-uṇḍ-uṇṇiyappam
ōṭi vāyōṭi vāyenn-uṇṇikkaṇṇā nin-
kālaṭi muttuvān vembalāyi
kālaṭi muttuvān vembalāyi

I prepared unniyappam (a kind of sweet) to give all Your friends. Come running, O my little Kanna! I long to kiss Your feet.

cemmē paśukkaḷe tēṭi-tteḷikkām ñān
kūṭṭukār-entinu nammaḷ pōrē
maṇṇappam cuṭṭu nī tannīṭum-eṅkilō
maṇṇum ñān tinniṭum uṇṇikkaṇṇā

When You take the cows for grazing, I will come. It's enough if only You and I go. No need for Your other friends. If you make a mud-cake and give it to me, I will eat even mud, O my little Kanna!

uḷḷil taḷattil-uriyilē pālkkuṭam
uṇṇikkuṭaykkuvān tanne veykkām
ōṭi vāyōṭi vāyen kaḷḷakkaṇṇā nin-
pūmēni pulkuvān vembalāyi
pūmēni pulkuvān vembalāyi

I will keep a pot of milk in my heart of hearts just for You to come and break! Come running, O my darling thief! I long to hug Your beautiful form.

tēḍi tēḍi (Tamil)

tēḍi tēḍi ōḍi vandēn kaṇṇapirānē – unnai
kāṇāmalē vāḍi nindrēn kaṇṇapirānē
māḍukaḷai mēykkavēṇḍi āsai koṇḍīrō
kāḍu malaikaḷellām suttri vandīrō

O Kṛṣṇa, I have run here and there in search of You. Unable to find You, I am dispirited. Did you want to take the cows for grazing? Or did you wander around the woods and hills?

anḍrorunāḷ draupadikku āḍai tandīrō
mattrorunāḷ maṇṇaittindru kāṭci tandīrō
pinnorunāḷ pāmbin mīdu āḍi nindrīrō
vēṇugānam seydu ennai makizhacceyvīrō

One day You lengthened Draupadi's sari indefinitely. On another day, You ate a mouthful of mud, and opened Your mouth to reveal the universe. On yet another day, You danced gracefully on the heads of the hydra-headed serpent and gladdened our hearts with sweet melody from Your flute.

karuṇaiyuḍan kāttiḍuvāy kaṇṇapirānē
annaiyum nī tandaiyum nī ādarippāyē

O Kṛṣṇa, be compassionate and protect us. You are our mother and our father. We worship You!

tērā darśan karnē (Punjabi)

jay kārā śērāvālīdā... jaykārā mērāvālīdā
jay kārā lāttāvālīdā... bōl sācē darbār dī jay

Victory to the Mother who rides the lion. Victory to the giver of boons. Victory to all the universe which is Your court.

tērā darśan karnē, tērā darśan karnē
mā tērā darśan karnē, tērā darśan karnē

We thirst for Your darshan, O Mother.

asī dūrō calkē āyē
tērā darśan karnē māyē
pērāvic pēgayē chālē
phirvi asi paj paj āyē
tērā darśan karnē, tērā darśan karnē

We have walked from far for Your darshan (Indian tradition of walking, climbing mountains to the holy temples of Ma Durga). Though our feet are blistered, we have come all the way.

kōl sānu bulāle mā
galē sānu lagālē mā
ik hōjāvāṅke phir mā jīv parmātmā

Call us close and embrace us, that our individual souls may be one with the Supreme.

ō tērā darśan... ōhō, ō tērā darśan... āhā
tērē darśan dē pyāsē mā, ō śērāvāli mā...
tērā darśan karnē, tērā darśan karnē...

We thirst for Your darshan, O Mother, who rides the lion. For Your darshan, O Mother.

mā tū avtār hai
terī karuṇā aparampār hai
pavsāgar tō pār karaṇ nu
kāphī tērā pyār hai

O Mother, You are a divine incarnation. Your compassion is incomparable. Your love is enough to carry us across the ocean of transmigration.

tērē vicc maiyā (Punjabi)

tērē vicc maiyā maiyā vicc tū
paramēhēsās jagālēy tū
paramānand dī amṛt dhārā vicc
rōmrōm jagālēy tū

"Mother is within you, you are within Mother." Awaken to this supreme Truth within you. May your every cell awaken in supreme bliss.

jis miṭinū... kuṭkuṭ hasēyā
ōmiṭī ik din hasēgī
jis jīvan tē mānhē tēynū
ik din lēykē vōhasēgī

O man, as the potter laughingly pats the clay, remember that one day the clay will also laugh. One day that clay will reclaim this body that you take such great pride in.

palpal dī kī... mat tū samajhī
palnā kōyī gavāyī tū

mādē karuṇā sāgar vicc
bandē līn hō jāyītū

O man, understand the value of every moment! Without wasting even a single moment, merge in that ocean of compassion.

The pendulum of life (English)

The pendulum of life swings back and forth
but the mind can be stilled by efforts put forth.
Practicing this, let me call out to you with love.

amma amma amma amma

Devotion to you, service to you
crying to you, praying to you—
By fixing my mind always on you
I'll see there's no distance between me and you.

The things of this world, in a moment disappear.
What is forever ours is already so near.
Remembering this, let me call out to you with love.

Despite all my efforts, like a drop in the sea,
your grace is what counts when death comes for me.
Knowing this, let me call out to you with love.

The world reels (English)

The world reels in the darkness of pain.
Past actions are choking us now.
Let us step out of this deep darkness
and light the small lamp of love.

Let's come together, let's come together.
Ignite the inner light—
a lamp of hope,
a lamp of compassion,
a lamp of unity.

How can I end this terrible darkness
with this tiny lamp of mine?
If each one lights the lamp of our hearts,
the world will sparkle and shine.

Let's come together, let's come together.
Ignite the inner light—
a lamp of goodness,
a lamp of knowledge,
a lamp of selflessness.

Let us lead a life of awareness
where no one is left behind,
where love will heal, both man and nature,
and wisdom will prevail.

Let's come together, let's come together.

Ignite the inner light—
a lamp of right thinking,
a lamp of right action,
a glow at the right time.

Divine Mother, Divine Mother!
Bless us with your grace.
where selfless action and compassion
guide us all the way.

tīn guṇōṅ kī (Hindi)

tīn guṇōṅ kī tērī kāyā
tīn guṇōṅ kī māyā
jag jīvan tū jaisā samjhē
tērē man kī chāyā

Your body is made of three gunas, and maya also consists of three gunas. How the world and life appear to you is your own mind's projection.

bandē... bandē...
bandē... bandē...

O Man...

khōj rahā bāhar tū jiskō
vāsī antar man kā
rūp samāyā ēkahi sab mēṅ
tūnē hī bilgāyā

What you seek outside is within you. A single Consciousness pervades all names and forms; it is you who create the differences!

tēri tṛṣṇā buntī rahtī
jāl tērē bharmōṅ kā
bhāv sabhī sukh-duḥkh kē prāṇī
upaj tērē karmōṅ kē

Only your desire weaves the web of your delusions. Your own actions produce your happiness and sorrow.

apnī mastī kā tū hī kāraṇ
tū hī khud kō rulātā
masti kē us ghaṭ kō ākhir
kāhē tū chalkātā

You alone cause your joy and you alone cause your misery. Why do you throw away the joy and happiness from your pot (of bliss)?

toṭṭuṇartti (Tamil)

toṭṭuṇartti en manadai kaṭṭiyiḍu tāyē
pattradanai nīkki māya kaṭṭ-avīzhttiḍāyō

By Your divine touch, please awaken my Self and restrain my restless mind. Won't you remove my attachments and release me from the shackles of illusion?

caraṇam tēḍi vandavarin iḍargaḷai takarttu nī
talaiyai tāzhttumbōdu abhaya karamtanai
uyarttuvāy
maruḷilē kiḍandu kālam iruḷaiyē vidaikkavō
arivilē amarndu tāyē oḷiyena tazhuvu nī

For those seeking refuge in You, You are the remover of obstacles. Only if the head bows down in reverence will You extend Your graceful hands in refuge. O Mother, I have been deluded for years. Should I continue wallowing in darkness? Will You not kindle knowledge in me and caress me with Your divine light?

janana-maraṇapiṇi bhayakkum arugil nī irukkavē
nigarillāda tāymaiyālē tuyargaḷai tuḍaikkavē
parama ātmaśaktiyāy irundu aruḷ pālikkum
janani nityakanniyē dariśanam tarum śāntiyē

When You are present, even the disease of birth and death will fear to come near. Your motherhood is unparalleled. You wipe away the tears of devotees. You are the Almighty who bestows grace. O Mother, O Eternal Virgin, the mere sight of Your divine form confers peace.

tuḷaśīmāḷā gaḷā (Marathi)

tuḷaśīmāḷā gaḷā ubhā viṭhōbā sāvḷā
paṇḍharī nāthā śrī raṅgā
viṭṭhal pāṇḍuraṅgā
viṭṭhal viṭṭhal pāṇḍuraṅgā viṭṭhal viṭṭhal pāṇḍuraṅgā

Lord Krishna, with His dark complexion, stands with a garland of tulasi around His neck. Victory to Lord Vithala, the Lord of Pandari and Sriranga!

bhakt puṇḍalikā gharī ubhā viṭṭhal viṭṭēvarī
avataralī karuṇā gaṅgā
jay jay viṭṭhal pāṇḍuraṅgā
viṭṭhal viṭṭhal pāṇḍuraṅgā viṭṭhal viṭṭhal pāṇḍuraṅgā

You stand on a brick in the house of Pundalika (a devotee). You are a Ganga of compassion. Victory to Lord Vithala, the Lord of Pandari and Sriranga!

ā ī rakhumāī vāmāṅgī candrabhāgā caraṇālāgī
santāciyā jīvalagā
jay jay viṭṭhal pāṇḍuraṅgā
viṭṭhal viṭṭhal pāṇḍuraṅgā viṭṭhal viṭṭhal pāṇḍuraṅgā

Mother Rukmini stands on your left. The river Chandrabhaga flows, touching Your divine feet, O Krishna, friend of the downtrodden. Victory to Lord Vithala, the Lord of Pandari and Sriranga!

śrīharī saguṇ sākār sarv sukhācē āgār
dēī bhaktisukh apār
jay jay viṭṭhal pāṇḍuraṅgā
viṭṭhal viṭṭhal pāṇḍuraṅgā viṭṭhal viṭṭhal pāṇḍuraṅgā

Sri Hari, is the very embodiment of good qualities. He is the treasure of all happiness and comfort. He grants us the delight of devotion within. Victory to Lord Vithala, the Lord of Pandari and Sriranga!

viṭṭhal viṭṭhal viṭṭhal viṭṭhal viṭṭhal viṭṭhal pāṇḍuraṅgā
viṭṭhal viṭṭhal viṭṭhal viṭṭhal jay jay viṭṭhal pāṇḍuraṅgā

Victory to Vithala, victory to Panduranga!

tūyi kālō (Bengali)

tūyi kālō mōśi mīkhē kāḷi
jāgōt bhōlāś kīśēr tōrē
jāniś nākō katośātō
ārtiṭākē śākār torē

O Kali, why do you wear dark soot, playing the game of illusion? Do you realise, O playful one, so many are crying for your mercy?

pāyēr nupur tālē tālē
kiśēr cōndē duliś rēmā
ki ānondē jogōt rōciś
kiśēr jāl rē buniś rōmā

Wearing your anklets, to what tune do you sway. In what joy do you create this world, O Ma. What web is this, O Roma.

ālō dhēkē kālō bhōniś
khēlā khēliś anontō kāl
śōṅśār ki dhādhāy jōrāś
ē tōr kī māyā jāl

You cover the light with your darkness. Till eternity you play. Why create this mystery of samsara? To what avail is this maya ?

ṣibēr śātē cukti kōrē
mukti ēbār dē mā dēkhi
tōr bhubhōn bhōrā bhālōbāśār
prōkāś bhōrā ruptā dēkhi

Now, O Ma, do make a pact for me with Shiva. Shower me with realization. In eternal form shall I witness the world of your divine bliss!

tyāga diyā tūnē (Hindi)

tyāga diyā tūnē vraja kō giridhar
bani mathurā tujhē pyāri rē
kal tak jō thī pyāri rādhā
āj bani kyōṅ parāyī rē

Giridhara, You have left Vrindavan. Now, Mathura has become dear to You. Until just yesterday, wasn't I Your "beloved"? But today, how is it that I have become like a stranger to You?

nisa dina tōḍī dahi kī maṭkī
tōḍ diyā āj dil kō rē
tērē liyē sab khēl hē giridhar
duḥkha na jānī mōrī rē

Everyday You broke pots of butter. Breaking my heart didn't seem much different to You. For You all this is but play; You know not my sorrow.

hē giridhārī hē avatārī
rādhā hṛdayavihārī

You who lifted up the mountain, You are the indweller of Radha's heart.

nirmmōhī jō tum hō giridhar
vraja kī yād na āyēgī
prāṇa nāth jō tum hō mērē
rādhā jī nahi pāyēgī

Dispassionate as You are, O Giridhara, memories of Vrindavan may not cross Your mind. O You who are the Lord of my life, Radha shall not want to live any longer without You by her side.

jaba chūṭhē mērē prāṇa hē giridhar

apnī muralī bajānā rē
muralī dhun kī dhārā mē prabhu
miṭ jāyē tērī rādhā rē

At least when I take my last breath, O Giridhari, please come and play Your flute. In the stream of the music of Your flute, let Your Radha merge in You.

ulagam oru pūntōṭṭam (Tamil)

ulagam oru pūntōṭṭam tannānē – tannānē
uyirgaḷellām pūkkūṭṭam tillālē – tillālē
vaṇṇa vaṇṇa pūkkaḷ pūkkum
vāzhkkaiyoru koṇḍāṭṭam
vāzhkkaiyoru koṇḍāṭṭam tannānē – tannānē
vāzhkkaiyoru koṇḍāṭṭam tillāle – tillāle

The world is a garden where all living beings are its many-colored blooming flowers and life is a celebration. Life is a celebration.

āḍippāḍi sirippōmē
anaivarumē magizhvōmē
annai kāṭṭum vazhiyinilē tannānē – tannānē
ānandamāy naḍappōmē tillālē – tillālē
ānandamāy naḍappōmē tillālē – tillālē

Let us sing, dance and laugh. Let us all be happy. Let us happily walk the path shown by Mother.

oru tāy makkaḷena
ulaga sēvai seyvōmē
ūrkkūḍi tēr izhuppōm tannānē – tannānē

onḍrāga vaḍam piḍippōm tillālē – tillālē
onḍrāga vaḍam piḍippōn tillālē – tillālē

Let us serve the world as the children of one Mother. Let us come together to pull the chariot of the Lord.

sevaiyadan magimaimikka
nōkkamadai maravādē
mānilamum mēnmai perum tannānē – tannānē
manadinilē tūymai varum tillālē – tillālē
manadinilē tūymai varum tillālē – tillālē

Remember the noble purpose of serving others, for the world will become a better place and the mind will become pure.

āḍiḍuvōm āḍiḍuvōm ānandamāy āḍiḍuvōm
pāḍīḍuvōm pāḍīḍuvōm paravasamāy pāḍīḍuvōm

We shall dance in joy. We shall sing blissfully.

ulakattin ādhāra (Tamil version)

ulagattin ādhāra poruḷ nīyammā
guṇam nirainduḷḷa vizhigaḷ tan oḷi nīyammā
taḷargintra idayattin abhayam ammā – ellā
arivirkkum ūṭrākum arivum ammā

aruḷvāyē adarkkāga anaittum nīyē
anaivarkkum abhayam un padamtān ammā
kanivirkkum kanivāna karuṇai nīyē
aruḷ mazhai koñcam pozhivāy nī aruḷāzhiyē

vāgiś nāgēś (Hindi)

vāgiś nāgēś dēvēś jinkē
pairōṅ paḍē prāpt hōtē kṛpādān
śailēndr-sā bhīm ākār vālā
tū hī mahādanti dēnā kṛpādān

Lord Ganesha, You shower grace on those who take refuge in You. You are mighty as a mountain. Your tusks symbolize wisdom and mercy. Please bless us with Your grace.

mahākāy hō gaṇādhīś tū kṛpāvāri rāśē
gaṇēśāya namaḥ gaṇēśāya namaḥ gaṇēśāya namaḥ ōm

O merciful Lord of the ganas (all beings in creation), we bow down to You, O Ganesha.

himācal mē jab tū karē bālalīlā
ṣaḍānan hamēśā tumhēṅ sāth dētā
hamāri taraph tū kabhī ḍāl dṛṣṭi
hamē śakti vidyā susampatti dījē

When You are playful and mischievous in the Himalayas, Your brother, Kartikeya, happily plays with you. Please look our way, and bestow on us strength, knowledge and prosperity.

prabhō vighnarāyā sabhī ēk tum hō
nijānand mēṅ tum sadā rājate hō
sadā duḥkha-santapt lōgōṅ pē tērī
kṛpā hō sadānand pāvē sabhī dēv

O Vighnaraya (remover of obstacles), You are ever immersed in bliss. May Your grace be upon all of us who are lost in the world of conflict and sorrow. Let us attain the height of bliss.

vānōrum (Tamil)

vānōrum vāzhttiḍum vēzha-mukhattōnē
tārāyō untāḷai maravā varam
vāzhvil kurai tīrum vēda mudalvanai
vaṇangiḍum aḍiyārai sērum nalam

O Elephant-faced One, You are worshipped by the gods. Give us a boon to remember your lotus feet. You are praised by the Vedas and remove life's illness. You grant well-being to those who worship You.

poruḷōḍu pukazhāram taruvāyē gaṇanāthā
aḷavillā aruḷmāri pozhivāyē gaṇanāthā
gaṇanāthā gaṇanāthā tuṇai nīyē gaṇanāthā
gaṇanāthā gaṇanāthā vinai tīrppāy aruḷāḷā

Give us the garland of wealth and fame. Shower your limitless grace on us, O Ganesha. You are our only refuge. Please remove our difficulties and sins.

manam onḍri unaipāḍa varuvāyē gaṇanāthā
mati-tannai teḷivākki maruḷ nīkkum gaṇanāthā
gaṇanāthā gaṇanāthā tuṇai nīyē gaṇanāthā
gaṇanāthā gaṇanāthā vinai tīrppāy aruḷāḷā

O Ganesha, come to us, who sing your praise with one-pointed mind. O Ganesha, You give clarity of intellect and remove our darkness. Ganesha, you are our only refuge. Please remove our difficulties and sins.

vattātta snēhattin (Malayalam)

vattātta snēhattinn-urava tēṭi
ammē ī maru-bhūvil-alaññiṭavē
oru snēha-gaṅgayāy cārattu-vannu nī
hṛdayam kuḷirkke puṇarnn-ozhuki

Mother, I wandered through this desert searching for the eternal spring of love. As Ganga, the sacred river of love, You flowed into my heart and cooled me in Your loving embrace.

nin prēma-tīrattu bhaktyā-anurāgiṇiyāy
virahārdra-cittayāy nilppū ivaḷ
jīvitamām maru-bhūvil nī ennenne
ēkayākki vidūre-akannu?
ēkayākki vidūre-akannu?

With longing devotion, I stand at the shore of your love. My heart grieves at this separation from you. Why did you leave me alone in the desert of life. Why did you go away?

annu-toṭṭ-innōḷam vyatha-pūṇḍu kēṇivaḷ
nin-mukham tēṭi alaññiṭunnu
nī ennil nirayunna ātma-svarūpam ennu
ariyuvān-ākāte andhayāy
ariyuvān-ākāte andhayāy

From that day onwards, I cry out in pain as I wander in search of You. I am blind to the truth that you are the Atma which fills me.

niśa-tan viri-māril vīṇ-uraṅgi-ivaḷ
pāzhāyat-etrayō janmam vṛthā
poypōya janma-sukṛtamāy-ammē ñān
nin tiru sannidhi vann-aṇaññu
nin tiru sannidhi vann-aṇaññu

I slept through many lives in the darkness of ignorance. Yet I reached Your sacred presence because of good deeds from past births.

nin-kṛpā-tīrttham pakarnn-uḷḷil-ānanda
prēma-varṣam coriññīṭuk-ammē
onnāy cērnnu layicciṭaṭṭe nityam
ānanda-sāgarē muṅgiṭaṭṭē
ānanda-sāgarē muṅgiṭaṭṭē

O Mother, let a shower of Your grace fill my heart with joy. May we become One, forever immersed in the ocean of bliss.

vāzhkeyenum paḍaku (Tamil)

vāzhkeyenum paḍagu
ulakamenum kaḍalil
alaimōdi taḍumāri uzhandrāḍudu
vazhiyariyā vēḷayilē
disaimāra nēriḍum
kalangarai veḷiccamāgum guruvaruḷē

The boat of life tosses about on the ocean of the world. Not knowing how to navigate, we move in the wrong direction. But the Guru's grace, shining like a beacon light, will show us the way.

uravendru palarum
sondamendru silarum
uṛavāḍi onḍrāgi payanamāgumē...
irankiḍum nērattilē
payanam seydavarē
uravendru nirkkāmal senḍriḍuvārē...

Our companions on the journey of life include many friends and a few relatives. When it is time to bid farewell, our travel companions will not stay with us just because they are related. They will go.

yāringu tuṇayē
evaringu kāvalē
ārudalāy illayē yārumē
karuṇai ozhugum kaṇgaḷ
anbāna-mozhikaḷ
guruvaruḷay aḍaikkalam namatākumē...

Who can support us? Who can protect us? No one can console us. The Guru's compassionate gaze and loving words are our only refuge.

ettanai karmavinai
palanūru janmangaḷ
attanayilum nizhalāga toḍarndiḍumē
pittamadai tirutti
manadonḍṛāy nirutti
metta mey jñānattil karaindiḍumē

The karmic consequences of countless lifetimes trail us like a shadow. When our obsession with worldly pleasures ceases and the mind becomes focused, the dawn of knowledge will dispel the darkness of past karmas.

vēlmurugā vēlmurugā (Tamil)

vēlmurugā vēlmurugā vēlmurugā vā
vēṇḍukirōm kāttiḍavē mālmurugā vā
ōmkārapporuḷ tannai uraittavan nīyē
ānkāram nīkki emakkaruḷ purivāyē

O Lord Vel Muruga, we pray for you to come. Please come and save us. You explained the meaning of the Pranava Mantra "Om" to Lord Shiva. Please bless us to eliminate our ego.

vānōrai asuraruḍan pōrkkaḷattilē
sēnādhipatiyāga kāttu ninḍṛāyē
kāmādi pagaivaruḍan pōriḍum emmai
vīzhāmal kāttaruḷvāy kanda-sāmiyē
kanda-svāmiyē enkaḷ sonda-sāmiyē
kanda-svāmiyē enkaḷ sonda-sāmiyē

As a commander-in-chief of the devas, you protected them in the war against the demons. We are fighting with the demons of our desires. Please protect us from falling for them. O Lord Kandasami, you are our God!

ōḍi ōḍi sērttadellām udavavillaiyē
kūḍi ingē vandavarum kūṭa illaiyē
pāḍi undan padam paṇindōm bhayamum illaiyē
tēḍi unnai śaraṇaḍaindōm kuraiyum illaiyē
kuraiyum illaiyē oru bhayamum illaiyē
kuraiyum illaiyē oru bhayamum illaiyē

Whatever material things we accumulated did not help us. Some of the people who were with us are gone. We sang your glories and humbly bowed at your holy feet, hence we have no fear. Having surrendered to you, we have no shortcomings and we have no fear.

vēl murugā vēl murugā vēl murugā vēl vēl
vēl murugā vēl murugā vēl murugā vēl vēl
vēl vēl vēl vēl vēl murugā vēl vēl

vinati hamare tune (Odiya version)

minatī mō na sunīḷu tiḷē rē kānhāyi
kī dōsa dēkhīlu mōra nakahu kipāīn

gopiṅkā ākuḷa dukha disilāni tōtē
brajaku tu kanhāyi rē pāsōrilu satē
tharē ā mō kānhā ā kāḷiyā sunā

dina nayīn āsē sañja āsayī ākāsē
kaha kāhīn galā syāma phērība kēbē sē
tharē ā mō kānhā ā kāḷiyā sunā

khyanika lāgī śrīmukha dēkhā mōtē syāma
tōha binu kēyunparī dharībī ē prāṇa
tharē ā mō kānhā ā kāḷiyā sunā

viḍarātta tāmara (Kannada version)

muduḍida tāvare moggammā nāninnu
hūvāgi araḷalu hātorevē
prabhāmayi jagadamba baḷigenna bandāga
praphullita ḷāgalu kādiruvē

ajñānāndha rāḍiyindali mūḍi
prabhegāgi anukṣaṇa tapisiruve
kambani miḍiyuta kaṭākṣapūrṇa
darśanakāgi hambalisi
ammā ammā...
darśanakāgi hambalisi

araḷade bāḍuva vidhi ennadāyite?
avanige baruvāse enagillammā
bēḍamma bēḍa marujanma enage
pādake maṇidu nā yācisuve
ammā ammā...
pādake maṇidu nā yācisuve

viṭhala viṭhala viṭhala viṭhala (Konkani)

viṭhala... viṭhala... viṭhala... viṭhala...
pāṇḍuraṅgālī kīrutī gāvūyā
sarvai gōṇḍu pōrāli mūrutī pōḷōvyā

Let us sing the glories of Vitthala and gaze upon His beautiful, darling form.

kāśi pītāmbara kāsuto mārṇu
toṇḍārī hāsāccē phūla phullovnu
anudina-bhajanēka kānu tō dīvnu
ānandāmṛta rasū tō pīvnu

He wears a yellow garment and the flower of His smile is in full bloom. Hearing our bhajans, He drinks from the nectar of bliss.

raṅgā pāṇḍuraṅga...
viṭhala... viṭhala... viṭhala... viṭhala...
viṭhala... viṭhala... viṭhala... viṭhala...

O Vitthala

niḍalārī lāylā kastūrī tīḷo
tuḷasīccē māḷā śōbhita gaḷō
aṅgāccō raṅgū āslyārī kāḷō
paḷōcaka pāvnā donnī dōḷō

He wears a sandalwood mark on His forehead. Adorned with a garland of holy Tulasi leaves, His true color is of dark hue. His form sanctifies our eyes.

ēkādaśī anī pakṣida jāgarū
hōḷtā dēvḷāntu bhakticcō sāgarū
vārakkarī bhajakālō-mēḷuhēraṅgā
daruśana-dīvnō rākha kṛpāḷu

During the Ekadashi fasting days, in shining temples, we see oceans of devotion. Thousands gather during the sacred Festival of Varakkari (Konkani festival of Karnataka in glory of Lord Vitthala). Do grace us with Your darshan, O Compassionate One.

viṭhal hari viṭhal nām gajari (Marathi)

viṭhal hari viṭhal nām gajari
nitya nām smaraṇ hōyi śuddhi antari

Chant the name of Vitthala incessantly. Remembering this Holy name, your inner being will be purified.

mādhav lakṣminārh bhaja śrīhari
bhakt-varada śrīraṅg muraḷi murāri
sāvḷā hā pāṇḍuraṅg vasē paṇḍari
rakhumāyi sahita viṭhal nām gajari
viṭhal hari viṭhal hari nām gajari

Chant the name of the bewitching Lord of Lakshmi, the bearer of the Flute who blesses his devotees. Chant the name of the dark-hued Lord Vitthala. Chant His name with the name of His beloved wife Rukmini. Chant Vitthal Hari Vitthal ceaselessly.

śrīdhara śrīrang śrīnivāsa rē
gōpihṛday nandalāl rāsvihāri
navanīt cōr harē kuñjavihāri
rakhumāyi sahita viṭhal nām gajari
viṭhal hari viṭhal nām gajari

O Krishna, You dwell in the hearts of the Gopis and You orchestrate the Ras Leela (Divine dance of Life). Chant the name of the butter thief, the One who enjoys His Leelas. Chant the name Vitthal Hari, Vitthal ceaselessly.

sādhusaṅgē kīrttani raṅgē narahari
nirākār brahm hōyi saguṇ sākāri

amita mahimā gāvūni pāvanakari
rakhumāyi sahita viṭhal nām gajari
viṭhal hari viṭhal nām gajari

Krishna, You are the one who sings along with the sages. The Unmanifested Absolute also manifests attributes. Sing the glories of the Lord. Chant His purifying name along with the name of Rukmini. Chant the name Vitthal Hari Vitthal ceaselessly

viṭhal viṭhal pāṇḍuraṅga
jaya hari viṭhal pāṇḍuraṅga

Chant the name Vitthal Panduranga. Victory to the Lord.

vittumundā (Telugu)

vittumundā ceṭṭumundā ēdi mundaṇṭē
bhūmi navvindi vāṭṭi uniki tānē annadī
talli mundā biḍḍa mundā evaru mundaṇṭē
jagadamba navvindi tānē talli annadī

When asked seed or tree, which came first? Earth smiled and said both tree and seed depend on earth for existence. When asked child or mother who came first? Divine mother laughed and said she is the mother of all beings.

anni ambē... antā ambē... unnadi jagadambē...

Divine mother is in all and everywhere. Divine mother is all-pervading consciousness. Divine mother alone exists.

alala pōṭi alala pōru alala ghōṣa cūsi
kaṭali navvindi vāṭi āsarā tānē annadī
manasumundā sṛṣṭi mundā ēdi mundaṇṭē
ātma navvindi antā unnadi tānē annadī...

Looking at competition, fight and noisy waves, Ocean roared and said all waves rise from it and end in it. When asked mind or creation, which appears first? Self (atma-consciousness) chuckled and said it (Self) pervades everything.

iccha nīvē... karttā nīvē... jñānamu nīvammā...

When asked mind or creation, which appears first? Self (atma-consciousness) chuckled and said it pervades everything.

jaḍamu nīvē... cētana nīvē... paramu nīvammā...

You are desire within us; You are the doer of everything. You are knowledge personified.

anni ambē... antā ambē... unnadi jagadambē...

Divine mother is in all and everywhere. Divine mother is all-pervading consciousness. Divine mother alone exists.

yadukulam (Malayalam)

yadukulam veṭiññu nī akaleyāyī
yamunaye marannu nī pōyitennō
karimukil mānattu kaḷiyāṭum nēram
iru-mizhiyitilallō nīr coriññu

You have abandoned Yadukula and gone far away. Have You even forgotten the Yamuna River? My eyes shed tears when rainclouds chase each other across the sky.

akaleyāy sandhyakaḷ uṭayāṭa ñoriyumbōḷ
aṇiyuvān kaṇṇā nī arikilillā
kuzhalviḷi kātilāy muzhaṅgumappōḷ
hṛdi tāḷam ninpada nisvanam-āyiṭum
gōpika ramaṇa nīlalōhitā... murahari nī śaraṇam
mēghavarṇṇa jaya vāsudēva jaya pāhipāhi
śaraṇam

The dusk weaves a colorful fabric but, Krishna, You are not near to wear them. The melody of Your flute resounds in my ears. The rhythm of Your footsteps is the tempo of my heartbeat. O darling of the gopis (milkmaids), Nilalohita, who destroyed the demon Mura, You are my refuge. Victory to the Lord whose complexion is like dark rainclouds. Victory to Vasudeva! I seek refuge in You.

vipināntarāḷattil vāsanta mārutan
alarkkula utirkkumbōḷ ōrttu-pōkum
vanamāla aṇiyuvān nīyillennākil
malaritin vāzhvukaḷ veruteyallē
gōpika ramaṇa nīlalōhitā... murahari nī śaraṇam
mēghavarṇṇa jaya vāsudēva jaya pāhipāhi
śaraṇam

I remember You when the spring breeze moves through the forest and flowers flutter gently to the ground. If You do not wear the garland of wild flowers, the lives of these blossoms will be in vain. O darling of the gopis (milkmaids), Nilalohita, who destroyed the demon Mura, You are my refuge. Victory to the Lord whose complexion is like dark rainclouds. Victory to Vasudeva! I seek refuge in You.

kusṛtiyōṭarikattāy kuzhal viḷiccaṇayumbōḷ
kuṇuṅgi kuṇuṅgi nī naṭam-āṭumbōḷ
irukaram cērttu nin-kaviḷiṇa mukaruvān
arutāte hṛdayam piṭacciṭunnu
gōpika ramaṇa nīlalōhitā... murahari nī śaraṇam
mēghavarṇṇa jaya vāsudēva jaya pāhipāhi
śaraṇam

You come to me as a mischievous boy playing the flute, and You enchant me with Your dance. My heart longs to hold Your face in my hands and kiss it tenderly. O darling of the gopis (milkmaids), Nilalohita, who destroyed the demon Mura, You are my refuge. Victory to the Lord whose complexion is like dark rainclouds. Victory to Vasudeva! I seek refuge in You.

www.ingramcontent.com/pod-product-compliance
Lightning Source LLC
LaVergne TN
LVHW051729080426
835511LV00018B/2953
* 9 7 8 1 6 8 0 3 7 8 5 0 4 *